FROM

BALTIMORE

BALTIMORE STEAM PACKET COMPANY

FOR THE CONVEYANCE OF PASSENGERS,
MERCHANDISE, SPECIE, BAGGAGE, ETC.

GOOD FOR ONE CONTINUOUS PASSAGE VIA

THE

OLD BAY LINE

1840-1940

NOT RESPONSIBLE FOR LUGGAGE. MEALS AND BERTHS
EXTRA. BANDS OF MUSIC WILL BE PROVIDED ON THE
STEAM BOATS FOR THE ENTERTAINMENT OF PASSENGERS.

Alexander Crosby Brown

Author.

BONANZA BOOKS · NEW YORK

TO

OLD POINT COMFORT
NORFOLK-PORTSMOUTH

To

A. C. B., JR. AND *B. J. B.*

WHO I HOPE WILL GROW UP TO FOLLOW
A LONG LINE OF FOREBEARS IN A LOVE
OF SALTWATER AND SHIPS.

Preface

LTHOUGH today there is often exhibited an unfortunate tendency to forget those forces which most tellingly combined to create and unify the United States of America into a nation, nevertheless sober analysis points to the development of transportation as being the most vital single factor which permitted this to come to pass. In the field of transportation the rôle of steam propelled craft is of paramount importance and it has been truthfully written that "the American steamboat knit the East and built the West."*

This country has been richly endowed by nature with broad, navigable rivers and deep, protected sounds which, like sparkling beads on a giant necklace, are dotted along the coast from Maine to Florida. At the beginning of the Eighteenth Century with no highways worthy of the name and settlements linked together only by sailing craft, pawns of wind and tide, it may be readily seen that the evolution of the steamboat as the *only* reliable and swift means of communication proved an inestimable boon. The meteoric development of steam-driven craft was in direct answer to the pressing need which first nurtured them into being.

Rivaling Long Island Sound in importance as a water link along our eastern seaboard, Chesapeake Bay, fed by more than a dozen broad rivers penetrating deep into the hinterland, has been since early times the theatre of the most spectacular developments in the maritime history of the nation. By its waters was fought the conclusive contest of Yorktown which insured at last the independence of the American Colonies. Later, in 1812, Chesapeake Bay and its tributaries again were the principally contested areas during our

---

*R. W. McAdam, *Salts of the Sound*, 1939, p. 15.

second struggle with the Mother Country. Again, and tragically so, the War of Secession brought the Chesapeake and its rivers into the limelight.

No less important has been the peace time rôle played by the Chesapeake. Her shipbuilders and mariners spread her fame throughout the world and wherever sailors congregated the famous Baltimore clipper became the byword for capability, seaworthiness, and speed. While her mariners on the high seas continued this splendid tradition, it is easy to appreciate why locally still another class of resourceful sailors came into being: the steamboatmen, for Chesapeake sea-folk were not long in recognizing the importance of craft with "tea-kettles" in them made to stem the tide.

Much has been said of the tremendously unifying influence of the railroad in this country, and it is true that the steel rails spreading ever westward have played a vitally important part. The railroads, however, came as the second step in the history of communications and it is significant to note that they were originally envisaged not as competition to the coastwise and river steamboat lines, but were designed to extend and complement them by pushing deeper into the surrounding country. Thus, the first railroads were feeders for the steamboats.

That anathema, speed, which first called steamboats into being, later turned on them with infanticidal fury, and in point of number steam craft today can not compare to their heyday of a generation or two ago. The original picture became reversed, rails controlled the ships and competition was to the death. For a long time the steamboat held its own until with trucks and motorbuses coming into the picture a great many of the famous old lines like the Bangor and Fall River were forced to suspend their services. *Sic transit gloria mundi:* cliché but true!

We have seen that in colonial days life was necessarily stately and slow. Travel even for the wealthy had little to recommend it, for when the jolting stage coach was mired down in knee-deep mud, passengers rich and poor alike had to put their shoulders to the wheel to get it out. The steamboat offered ease and elegance plus speeds hitherto believed impossible. With steam the great class of American tourists was born.

For those to whom speed was the prime requisite, the steamboat later was abandoned for the railroad, to be in turn diverted by the air transport. Fortunately for those who decry the passing of a slower, more gracious living, there is a movement to reclaim the calm of Colonial days. Many ask themselves the need for hurry, the tempo of modern life is already geared too high for health or comfort. With this sane trend made manifest, the safe and comfortable steamboat is reasserting itself, for unlike any other existing means of travel, a ship affords its passengers three-dimensional space in which to move, a pleasant contrast to the virtually one-dimensional corridor of the train, or the no-dimensional seat on plane or bus.

For any organization to have survived throughout the varying economic picture for the past century would surely indicate that it was not only well grounded in the first place, but that those in whose charge its destinies have lain were particularly adept at meeting new situations and readjusting to conform to changing times. It is not strange that Chesapeake Bay, a principal artery of life-blood of the nation, should have given birth to what is today the oldest active steamboat company in existence in America. The Baltimore Steam Packet Company, now familiarly known as the Old Bay Line, has for a century run steamers up and down the Chesapeake, gateway between North and South. Unique in the pageant of America's water-borne commerce, the Old Bay Line, whose history we shall trace in the following pages, in rounding out its centennial of faithful and constant service to the American public occupies an enviable position in the annals of American enterprise.

There is an old sea chanty sung in bygone days by sailors of Chesapeake Bay's famous Baltimore Clippers. It carries the lilting refrain:*

---

*J. C. COLCORD, *Songs of American Sailormen,* 1939, p. 67-8.
Also, W. B. WHALL, *Sea Songs and Shanties,* 1910, p. 137.

> A hundred years on the Eastern Shore,
> O yes O,
> A hundred years is a very long time!
> A hundred years ago.
>
> A hundred years have passed and gone
> O yes O,
> And a hundred years will come once more
> A hundred years ago.

Perhaps geologically or astronomically speaking the centenary period is insignificant, but when applied to shipping it may be truly said that "a hundred years is very long time!" Of the many steamship operators in the United States today only a small proportion may trace their existence back into the past century. Congratulations, therefore, to the patriarch of the tribe! We trust that "a hundred years will come once more."

For the historian, the compilation of a record of this kind is not as easy a task as might be first imagined. Source material has proved both scarce and elusive. Four times during the hundred years we will attempt to span, the Company has had valuable old records destroyed, three times by fire, once by flood. The search for material on the Line has been, however, both pleasant and rewarding. A sketch of one Old Bay Line steamboat turned up in London, details of another have come from San Francisco: such have proved the ramifications in tracking down the events and personalities of the company's story.

It would be superfluous to point out that this chronicle could not have been accomplished without the very real and generously awarded help of a great many people. I wish to acknowledge my initial debt of gratitude to my colleagues at The Mariners' Museum and to thank its president, Mr. Homer L. Ferguson, for his continued interest and encouragement. Miss C. W. Evans, librarian, contributed much aid and Mr. William T. Radcliffe took inestimable pains over the photographs reproduced herein. Mr. Thomas C. Skinner's map speaks for itself.

Officials of the Line itself have been tireless in their efforts to put material at my disposal and generous in their appreciation. Mr. Legh R. Powell, Jr., president of the Baltimore Steam Packet Company, has supplied the introduction which launches the book on the uncharted waters ahead; Mr. Robert E. Dunn, vice-president in charge of operation, has given unstintingly of his time and good nature; and of Mr. Raymond L. Jones, general passenger agent, it may be truthfully stated that but for him this book would have been still-born. Thanks go, too, to Mr. E. P. Hook, general agent; Mr. W. Andrew Miller, port engineer; Mr. P. S. Gornto, Norfolk general agent; and to officials of the Seaboard Air Line Railway at Norfolk and Portsmouth.

My list should likewise mention the kindness of Messrs. John W. and Watson E. Sherwood, sons of the late Captain John R. Sherwood, president of the Line for many years, and of his daughter Mrs. Perry Fuller.

My good friends, Messrs. John Philips Cranwell and James W. Foster, of Baltimore have both been of more assistance than they may realize, the former for a careful search through Baltimore Customs House records and the latter for his great help at the Pratt Library. Mr. Robert W. Parkinson supplied useful data on the San Francisco ferry *Calistoga,* ex-Old Bay Liner *Florida.* It is a pleasure also to acknowledge the invaluable assistance afforded by Mr. Elwin M. Eldredge, who probably knows more about American steamers than any living person, and who has used this knowledge to assemble one of the best collections of ship portraits in this country.

In addition to Mr. Eldredge, the following individuals and institutions have generously aided me with pictures and permission to use them: The Mariners' Museum, Newport News, Va.; the Enoch Pratt Free Library, Baltimore; the Municipal Museum of the City of Baltimore; the U. S. National Museum, Washington, D. C.; the National Maritime Museum, Greenwich, England; and the Peabody Museum, Salem, Mass.

Mr. J. B. Hunter, naval architect of Bethlehem Steel Company's

Quincy shipbuilding plant, furnished copies of drawings of old vessels constructed by Harlan and Hollingsworth; Mr. F. A. Hodge sent pictures of Sparrows Point ships; Mr. Daniel J. Brown of Pusey and Jones Shipbuilding Corporation sent photographs of the modern Bay Line steamers. Mrs. W. G. Lane furnished a photograph of her late husband, Mrs. W. W. Morgan lent a portrait of Capt. L. B. Eddens, Mrs. Franklin James a miniature of her father, Chief Engineer T. J. Brownley, and Miss Laura E. Hartge contributed a photograph of her grandfather, one of the Line's captains during the Civil War. Miss Audrey W. Davis, gave permission to reproduce a painting of one of the early side-wheelers. Mr. Richard D. Steuart lent me an old broadside covering the wreck of the *Medora*. Captain R. Sidney Foster, with whom I have enjoyed many delightful trips on the Bay, has given me not only a fund of information about the Line, but also photographs of his kinsman, the late Captain W. J. Bohannon, and of himself. Captain John L. Marshall likewise has been a pleasant companion of many voyages and has supplied much interesting data.

Thanks are tendered also to Dr. E. G. Swem, librarian of William and Mary College, and editor of the *W. & M. Quarterly,* for permission to use material originally published in that magazine, and to Mr. August Dietz, Jr., for his invaluable assistance in the production of the present volume.

In research material I have drawn extensively on files of Baltimore's great newspapers, the *American* and the *Sun,* made available at both the Pratt Library and the Maryland Historical Society. Mr. Edgar Ellis, librarian of the *Sun,* kindly placed references in my hands taken from his index. Books by Messrs. Fred E. Dayton, John H. K. Shannahan, and Roger W. McAdam have shed interesting light on the history of American steamboating. Dimensions and particulars of vessels mentioned herein are taken largely from the *U. S. List of Merchant Vessels,* inaugurated in 1868 and published annually by the Department of Commerce, Washington, D. C. For early vessels I am dependent on records made available by the

National Archives, Washington, D. C., and the Baltimore Customs House.

The roman numeral in brackets which appears after the names of a great many of the steamers is to differentiate them from others of the Old Bay Line which were built later on and given an identical name. It does not mean that the registered name of the ship in question included such numerals, but they should prevent confusion in the identities of the various boats.

Many other people have contributed in one way or another to the preparation of this story, but the place of honor is reserved for that great host of sailors, shipwrights, officials, passengers, engineers, and shippers alike, who without realizing it, have for these hundred years been making the history of the Old Bay Line. I have merely tried to write some of it down before it is forgotten.

A. C. B.

The Mariners' Museum
Newport News, Virginia
March 18, 1940.

The *President Warfield*. From a photograph taken in Baltimore Harbor in 1939.

Table of Contents

List of Illustrations

(End paper map by Thomas C. Skinner)

Introduction

O round out one hundred years of continued operation and service is, in and of itself, a notable accomplishment for any business. When it is realized that this record has been achieved in a nation which is only one hundred sixty-four years old, the accomplishment takes on even greater lustre and distinction.

Such is the record of the Baltimore Steam Packet Company, which in the maturity of its years has earned the name of "Old Bay Line." In this year of 1940, the Company celebrates its Centennial, marking one hundred years of continued operation on Chesapeake Bay. Founded in 1840, the Old Bay Line has grown up with the young nation which was only in its swaddling clothes at the time the Line came into being.

That the Company would become an institution was to be expected. It was founded upon the ideal of greater service to more people and it is impossible to measure the influence it has exerted during the last century upon the manners and customs of the territory. The imagination is stimulated by the thought of the new possibilities which its coming opened up for the inhabitants of the then sparsely settled communities and cities for which it provided a new and then ultra modern type of service. The extent to which it aided progress can not be stated in terms of mere dollars and cents. One must look beyond material values to gain an appreciation of the part the Old Bay Line played in the upbuilding of its territory and the fostering of interchange, both commercial and social, between the peoples of the areas it linked.

This book tells a story of men and ships—strong men and staunch ships. Through its pages there breathes again the spirit of those who founded the Company and the ideals of service which they conceived and which their successors have perpetuated through the succeeding ever-changing and kaleidoscopic years. How well those pioneers builded may best be judged by the enduring qualities of what they built.

Growth and progress have brought many changes to the Old Bay Line through the passing years. The transition from the Steamship *Georgia* of 1840 to the modern *President Warfield* of today did not come overnight. During the intervening years, this nation has been four times at war, business depressions have come and gone, marked changes have taken place in the manners and customs of the country —but, whether in times of peace or times of war, whether in times of plenty or times of need, the Old Bay Line has continued unfalteringly to fulfill its mission, the furnishing the year round of an assured and economical means of transportation between the lower and upper reaches of Chesapeake Bay.

What testimonial more fitting than that record could be chosen for those forward-looking, public-spirited men who, a century ago, formed the Company and laid the foundations upon which it has grown from year to year! No matter the troubled times—whether the vicissitudes of war, panic or other calamity—which have confronted the Company, the same faith that inspired those men a hundred years ago has given courage to succeeding managements to strive for the high objectives set by the founders.

So this book is presented as a tribute to those whose vision and courage brought into being a new business enterprise, one destined to become a great instrumentality in shaping the course of the region it served, a potent influence in the business and social life of its contemporaries. Their work is memorialized in the most splendid of all ways—in a living creation that has withstood the tests of time!

Grateful acknowledgment is made to Mr. Alexander Crosby Brown, Corresponding Secretary of The Mariners' Museum, Newport News, Virginia, and a former blue-water sailor, for his untiring efforts and interest in compiling this book. The vast amount of work involved in making a search through the records of a century may well be imagined, and it is only through Mr. Brown's diligence that this book has become a reality. The book, however, more than speaks for itself, and certainly its readers also will be deeply appreciative of the painstaking research the author conducted in order to give them so vivid and realistic a description of some of the high spots of the Old Bay Line's first hundred years of operation.

LEGH R. POWELL, JR.
President.

LEGH R. POWELL, JR.,
President, Baltimore Steam Packet Co.

ROBERT E. DUNN,
Vice-President and Operating Head of the Old Bay Line.

Via Old Bay Line in 1840

CHAPTER I

A CENTURY ago an anonymous traveler penned the following superlatively flowery description, which after cautioning our readers to take a deep breath, we will quote verbatim:*

The trip from Baltimore down the Chesapeake, in the fine steamer *Georgia,* was a delightful one. I have often heard old sea-captains, who have traversed almost every known sea, lake, bay, and river in the world, speak in the most exalted terms of the noble Chesapeake. As a bay it has no equal, not even in that of Naples, all things considered. I know of no more delightful trip, especially in the summer· season. Mine, on this last occasion, was particularly so. I emerged from the confines of a hot, murky city, and was soon out upon the broad blue waters, with an exquisite breeze, which came up with invigorating freshness from the silver waves. Night came on, and her azure curtain, gemmed with myriad stars, was drawn over the expanse above. A little while longer, and the pale moon, with her round modest face, peered up the eastern horizon. She looked like a sylvian queen gently blushing to take the place of her lord and master, who had just sunk from his majestic career behind a golden halo.

A scene on the Chesapeake, thus changing from noon-day to gray eve, thence to dim twilight, and deepening into the soft azure of a summer's night, is truly inspiring alike to the poet and painter, as well as invigorating to health, and renovating to the finer feelings of sentimentality and romance.

While our unnamed voyager, to whom we will refer hereafter as "Mr. Smith," is comfortably reclining on the after-deck of the "fine steamer *Georgia"* reveling in the sublime scene which he has painted for us and complacently permitting his "finer feelings" to have their way with him, let us leave him for a minute and look about the noble

---

*Quoted in W. S. FORREST, *Historical Sketches of Norfolk and Vicinity,* 1853, p. 456.

packet which is speeding him southward at the awesome rate of ten miles per hour. Mr. Smith had booked passage on the *Georgia*[I], flag-ship of the new line plying between the ports of Baltimore and Norfolk, and although he has intimated that he had made the trip before, nevertheless on that sunny day a hundred years ago he had his carriage deliver him and portmanteau at Spears Wharf, Baltimore, well in advance of the scheduled 4:00 P. M. departure. Snugly secured to her dock, the good ship *Georgia* resplendent in her coat of white paint, glistened in the afternoon light.

With ample time to kill, our Mr. Smith must have walked on down the wharf, leaned against a weather-worn spile and taken in to the fullest the animated scene before him. Heavy teams groaning under loads of bales, crates, and boxes surged through the dusty thoroughfare. Perspiring stevedors loaded piles of merchandise on hand trucks and rolled them over swaying gangways into the darkened doorways piercing the side of the *Georgia*. Ladies in billowing dresses picked their way gingerly across the road leaning heavily on the arms of their escorts respendent in stove-pipe hats and flowery waistcoats of watered silk. Dusky porters in white coats and caps bearing the legend "Bay Line" surrounded each approaching carriage, obsequiously bowed out the travelers and whisked away their luggage. In the background, "runners" of the rival "Upper Route" would hint darkly to all who would listen of the alledged dangers of steamboat travel and urge travelers to go on in safety to Washington in the "cars."

There was a constant din and the babel of many voices rent the air. Officers on the ship were calling instructions to their seamen; teamsters were shouting to the struggling horses; dock hands and stevedores lightened labor with song; small boys darting under foot yelled to one another; and hawkers impetuously cried the merits of their wares. Suddenly the shrill note of the *Georgia's* new-fangled steam whistle resounded and Mr. Smith consulted his heavy gold watch and decided that it was time he went aboard. Picking his way over to the passenger gangway he mounted in time to catch a startled "oh" from the lady passenger immediately preceding him who had looked down as she climbed the steps to the dark strip of water separating ship from shore. At the head of the gangway, Mr. Smith nodded to a fine frock-coated figure who could be none other than that doughty mariner, Captain James Coffey, master of the noble *Georgia*.

He surrendered his ticket to another resplendent figure, Mr. Wilson, ship's "Clerk," as pursers were then termed, and made his way to the upper deck to watch the late arrivals come aboard. Another impetuous blast of the steam whistle rent the air and white-coated stewards were now calling "All ashore that's going ashore."

The last few passengers had hurried across the gangplank when a team of lively horses pranced up to the dock and canvas bags were tossed from the wagon and whisked aboard. The "Great Southern Mail," just arrived from Philadelphia, had been delivered and now the *Georgia* was ready to begin her 200-mile voyage down the length of Chesapeake Bay. Lines were cast off as Captain Coffey, speaking trumpet in hand, took his place on top of one of the giant paddle boxes. The gilded wooden eagle surmounting the pilot house stood ready, poised for flight.

Crisp orders were given and suddenly the paddle wheels began to revolve and the proud steamboat slowly drew away from her dock. Gaining way, she headed straight out into the crowded channel as Spears Wharf and the waving figures on it diminished and became gradually lost from view.

Probably Mr. Smith was still in no hurry to go down to find his cabin as the various sights and sounds of the harbor must have held his attention. By the Lazaretto they passed the steamer *Patuxent* of Captain Weems' Rappahannock River Line, whose churning paddles marked a wake of creamy water far behind her. A fleet of graceful pungy schooners, some with watermelons piled high on deck, were sailing up the Patapsco, their snowy canvass, and rose pink sides forming variegated patterns against the foil of blue water and green slopes behind.

We will assume that with reluctance Mr. Smith at last tore himself from his place at the rail and made his way down to the Gentlemen's Saloon to claim his "birth," as it was then frequently spelled. Coming from the brilliant sunshine outdoors, he was momentarily blinded until his eyes became accustomed to the dimmer light within. Tiers of bunks lined the sides of the richly carpeted cabin and Mr. Smith assisted by a steward deposited his luggage in the space assigned to him by lot. By this time several convivial spirits had assembled around the bar and although his appetite had already been whetted by the salt air, Mr. Smith decided that he would partake of a julep as forestaste of the hospitality of the South whither he was bound.

Supper was now in order and although the dining saloon was below on a deck devoid of portholes, the meal was a cheerful one with white napery and silver glistening in the light cast by whale-oil tapers.

Gaining the deck again, Mr. Smith sought a chair on the open after-deck and fell into conversation with a naval officer and his wife who, he learned, were bound for Portsmouth where the officer was to be attached to the Gosport Navy Yard. He had noted on his way through the saloon that several card games were in progress and although he would have enjoyed whiling away an hour or so at whist, he sensibly decided that playing cards with strangers particularly on steamboats was a little risky.

The officer and his lady retired early and Mr. Smith stretching out comfortably in his chair was left to the musings he outlined for us when we left him. Obviously pleased with his lot Mr. Smith probably sat up on deck late drinking in the pleasant sights, smells, and sounds, being reluctant to exchange them for the discomforts of a narrow mattress in the stuffy cabin below. The paddle wheels continued their rhythmic slapping, waves danced in the moonlight, and the phosphorescent wake stretched in a straight line out astern. Clouds of black smoke burst from the tall black funnel that was the *Georgia's* crowning feature and occasionally showers of gleaming sparks burst forth to rival, as undoubtedly Mr. Smith himself would have expressed it, the Milky Way. Up through the fiddley wafted the smell of steam and hot oil and he could hear the distant clanking of machinery and the almost continual thud of heavy pitch-pine logs which the stokers were tossing from bunker to boiler.

Most of his fellow passengers had by this time either gone below or were sleeping out on deck with coats drawn over them. Occasionally sailors passed persuing their various duties and at periodic intervals, Mr. Smith could hear the lookout striking the ship's bells and reporting all well. Off on the horizon shone the emerald and ruby lights of passing ships and on the starboard hand the yellow gleam of a light-house marked a harbor's mouth.

With a sigh, Mr. Smith at last must have pulled himself from his chair, knocked out his pipe, and, realizing that he had a busy day ahead of him in Norfolk, gone down to bed.

Since we are privileged to look ahead a hundred years into the future, while Mr. Smith sleeps let us contrast the fine specimen of naval architecture called the *Georgia* with the steamers on which he might have traveled today. We are afraid that the little *Georgia,* noble steam packet though she was for her times, would be dwarfed to insignificance by her modern sisters. Measuring almost twice as long, and with engines twenty times more powerful, the modern screw-driven craft built of resistant steel, steam silently along with oil burning under their massive boilers. Passengers have well appointed staterooms, electric lights, and running water: a decided contrast to the *Georgia's* dimly lit cabins and crude washing facilities. If during the night the ministrations of a steward were required, Mr. Smith would have had to search the corridors in his nightshirt till he found one, today he would have merely touched the electric bell.

These and similar contrasts being obvious, let us take a good look at the little *Georgia*. John Robb of Baltimore had been her builder and she had been launched in 1836, four years before the Baltimore Steam Packet Company came into being and took over her ownership. Her wooden hull was strongly built of tough red cedar and locust, for the *Georgia* was designed as a sea-boat for the Atlantic Line on the exposed run from Norfolk to Charleston around treacherous Cape Hatteras. She measured 551 tons and was 192 feet in length, by 24 feet beam, and 12.2 depth. Her planks were secured to staunch ribs with copper fastenings and her bottom was covered with copper sheathing as a protection against marine borers.

Charles Reeder had built her 140 horse-power steam engine, the typical lever-beam type with a single upright cylinder measuring almost four feet in diameter from which plunged a piston with 9½ foot stroke. Above was placed on a massive wooden gallows frame the cast-iron walking beam which took the power from the piston and transferred it to the paddle shaft. Heavy copper boilers, fired by logs, furnished low pressure steam. Slowly turning paddle-wheels drove her through the water, but when the inevitable breakdown occurred, she could resort to spreading sails. Modern Bay Line steamers have radio telephones, but if a mishap occurred to the *Georgia,* she had to make her way alone. "A new and superior steam packet" was how they described her back in 1836,* when Captain William Rollins first conned her out of Norfolk harbor en route to the South Carolinian port, and passengers on the line were reassured by the announcement that:† "the captain is well acquainted with the coast and the engineers are approved practical men."

We have seen that Mr. Smith's berth was one of a number arranged in tiers along the sides of the main saloon aft. In another part of the boat was situated the mirrored and begilded "Ladies' Cabin" from which men were excluded thus separating man and wife traveling together. A smaller cabin was situated forward of the machinery and similarly equipped with curtained berths. Some of the steamboats of the line had three or four staterooms on deck; the modern equivalent would be the cabins de luxe and the bridal suites.

---

*Baltimore *American,* Nov. 3, 1836.
†Richmond *Compiler,* Oct. 24, 1834.

Meanwhile as Mr. Smith was sleeping soundly on his narrow shelf while insomniacs tossed to the accompaniment of their more fortunate companions' snores, the *Georgia* plowed along through the night. Her voyage half completed she passed her running mate on the line, the smaller side-wheeler *Jewess* commanded by Captain Thomas Sutton, northbound for Baltimore.

The first gray streaks of approaching dawn found her skirting a fleet of fishermen in sailing canoes outward bound for the day's work on York Spit shoals. She plowed steadily onward to meet short choppy seas washing over the Horseshoe, as the ebb tide ran counter to the gentle Sou-wester sweeping off the land. Soon she rounded Thimble Shoals and made her way westward toward the mouth of Hampton Roads. The dock at Old Point Comfort lying below the guns of recently completed Fortress Monroe awaited and already some sleepy-eyed passengers who were getting off to stay at the Hygeia Hotel for the "bathing season" at the new resort were about on deck.

The clamor attendant to bringing the *Georgia* alongside the wharf undoubtedly woke Mr. Smith and his companions and after waiting his turn to dip his face in a basin of cold water, he quickly dressed and went on deck.

A heavy tide-rip ruffled the water and the *Georgia* tossed uneasily, straining against the hawsers which bound her to the land. Meanwhile several passengers had gone ashore, some to stay at the resort, others to transfer to the steamboat *Thomas Jefferson* which was tied up ahead of the *Georgia* bound for James River landings, City Point, and Richmond.

As soon as the last box of cargo had been left ashore, the *Georgia's* whistle blared, she fell back on her spring line, the paddles churned, and she was off on the last leg of her voyage across Hampton Roads and up the Elizabeth River to the thriving port of Norfolk. The Roads was full of ships: lofty clippers homeward bound from South America and the Orient; sailing packets, every stitch of canvas drawing as they skirted the Rip Raps bound for the harbors of the world; glistening white steamboats like the *Georgia* belching forth clouds of gray smoke; busy side-wheel steam tugs towing strings of deeply laden barges.

Mr. Smith hated to miss anything that was going on, but his empty feeling inside had to be first satisfied and shortly after the boat had cleared the Old Point dock, her passengers assembled at the breakfast table.

A little over an hour later the *Georgia* threaded her way up river and nudged in to her dock lying in the center of the busy town. Mr. Smith cast a last quick glance around the harbor. Across the water and beyond the town of Portsmouth on the opposite bank, he could pick out the tall spars of U. S. Navy frigates lying by the Gosport Yard. Directiy opposite he could see the wharves to which the *Georgia* would soon repair, the passenger cars and puffing locomotive of the Portsmouth and Roanoke Railway already waiting to speed on southward (at ten miles an hour) those of the *Georgia's* company who had booked through passage. With mixed feelings our sentimental friend then turned his back on the scene, seized his portmanteau, and stepped down the gangway to the land. His trip via Old Bay Line a century ago was done.

Genesis

CHAPTER II

LTHOUGH the steamboats of a century ago were by no means the efficient and capable craft of today, nevertheless, when the Baltimore Steam Packet Company was organized in 1839, steamboats were no novelty on Chesapeake Bay. Before taking up the main thread of our story on the Old Bay Line, it would be well to review the history of steam navigation on the Bay for the twenty-five-year period prior to the Baltimore Steam Packet Company's coming into being.

First an attempt should be made to refute the popularly accepted myth to the effect that Robert Fulton, genius though he undoubtedly was, invented the steamboat. Many years before Fulton's *Clermont* steamed up the Hudson River, inventors had built and operated steam driven craft in both this country and abroad. One of these men, James Rumsey, had built a successful vessel on the Potomac River in which George Washington was interested. John Fitch, misunderstood and ridiculed, at the same time built a series of steamboats both in New York and Philadelphia. Fulton, however, combined mechanical skill with practical business acumen, and his *Clermont* was unquestionably the first commercially successful steam craft. The *Clermont* made her bow in 1807, was rebuilt and lengthened the following year, and was then followed by the *Paragon, Car of Neptune,* and other steamboats, each superior to its predecessor. Permanently established steamboat services having germinated in the waters of New York spread rapidly throughout the country. On June 8, 1808, John Stevens' celebrated *Phoenix,* debarred by the Fulton-Livingston monopoly, was taken around the Jersey coast by

Capt. Moses Rogers and placed in service on Delaware Bay and in so doing effected the first ocean voyage of a boat propelled by other than man-power or the wind.

Baltimore's first steamer was the *Chesapeake,* built in 1813 at Flannigan's Wharf by Captain Edward Trippe.* Discounting Rumsey's experimental craft of the previous century, the *Chesapeake* was the first commercial craft to ply the waters for which she had been named. Two members of the syndicate which built her, Andrew F. Henderson and General William McDonald, should be especially singled out here, for a quarter of a century later these men were among the incorporators of the Baltimore Steam Packet Company, Henderson serving as its first president and McDonald as a director.

The *Chesapeake* was especially constructed as a link in the transportation service between Philadelphia and Baltimore. The Delaware and Chesapeake Canal was not due to be dug for another fifteen years and the then accustomed route of the south-bound traveler consisted of boarding a sailing packet at Philadelphia for the trip down Delaware Bay to Newcastle; thence via swaying stage coach across the upper neck of the Delmarva Peninsula where at Frenchtown the traveler again embarked on a sailing packet for the trip down the Elk River across the head of the Chesapeake and up the Patapsco River to Baltimore. This region is notorious for its calms and transportation was both slow and uncertain. As soon as the builders could have her ready the *Chesapeake* was placed on the Baltimore-Frenchtown run on what became known as the Union Line.

The dispatch with which the *Chesapeake* could traverse this route made it impossible for sailing packets to compete with her, and two years later the rival Briscoe-Partridge Line running to Elkton secured a little 110-foot steamboat the *Eagle,* built in Philadelphia in 1813, which had been brought around by sea from the Delaware to the Virginia Capes. Her trip under the command of

---

*See also J. H. K. SHANNAHAN, *Steamboat'n' Days,* 1930, p. 9.

Captain Moses Rogers, (as we have seen Rogers was first master of the *Phoenix* and was later called to the command of the auxiliary steamship *Savannah* on her trans-Atlantic voyage in 1819) marked the initial appearance of the steamboat at sea below Cape Henlopen and she was also the first steamboat at the lower end of the Chesapeake. In traversing the route from lower to upper Bay in 1815, the *Eagle* blazed the trail which now, 125 years later, is followed by steamers of the Old Bay Line and the latter may trace their ancestry back without break to this memorable little craft—the first Norfolk-Baltimore steamer.

If the *Georgia,* first boat of the Old Bay Line, on which our Mr. Smith took passage, seemed crude compared to their modern craft, what of the little *Eagle?* We have stated that she was only 110 feet in length. Her width was less than 20 feet and her cumbersome machinery and boiler which occupied the best part of the hull was placed slightly forward of amidships so that the distance from her bow to her paddle wheel shaft came to 46 feet. Her wooden hull was closely patterned after those of sailing packets, and like them, she was steered by a long tiller aft. A tall mast from which a square-sail could be set was placed foreward of the machinery. Proceeding aft, next came the cumbersome paddle wheels shrouded by their protecting guards astride which stood the massive cross-head of her elementary "steeple" engine. Fire-room and boiler surmounted by its smudgy smoke-stack came next, while the entire after part of the deck was covered by a tent-like awning. Below this was the "great" cabin which served as dining and sleeping quarters for her passengers and which was mainly ventilated by a row of windows piercing her square transom stern. There was no pilot house and Captain Moses Rogers, stove-pipe hat firmly planted on his head, conned her from the top of one of the paddle-boxes, bellowing instructions to his quarter-master aft, or climbing down to stamp on deck as signal to his engineers.

Although the *Eagle* was employed mostly on the Baltimore to Frenchtown run, she made several trips down the Bay to Norfolk and in July 1815 she steamed up the James to Richmond, making the round trip back to Baltimore in a week.

The *Eagle* was short lived, however, even for those times and on April 18, 1824, her boiler exploded killing a passenger, Henry M. Murray, and injuring Captain George Weems who was then operating her on the route to Annapolis and the Patuxent River. According to the historian, T. W. Griffith,* this melancholy occurance marked the first steamboat fatality on the Bay.

Following the *Chesapeake* and a companion craft on the Union Line, the *Philadelphia,* the third Baltimore built steamboat was the packet *Virginia.* The *Virginia* was the first steamer to have been expressly built for the Baltimore and Norfolk service and was contemporaneously described as being "a very large and staunch boat, elegantly fitted."† It is interesting to note that to achieve this distinction in the year 1817 some $55,000 were spent on her construction, just about one-twentieth of what it would cost to built a vessel suitable for the trade today.

As first built (she was later lengthened) the *Virginia* measured 136 feet long, by 24 feet 9-inch beam, by five-foot draft. Her arrangement and method of construction was similar to the *Eagle,* but her machinery was larger and more efficient. William Flannigan built the hull and Watchman & Bratt the engine. This was of the low pressure "steeple" type and had a single cylinder of 35-inch diameter by four-foot stroke, achieving 44 horse power at 18 revolutions per minute of the paddle shaft. Her boiler was of shining copper and therefore of greater longevity than the less expensive cast-iron ones, for in those days ordinary sea-water was made into steam leaving a clogging residue of salt. In order to keep up her normal of eight pounds steam pressure she burned between twenty and twenty-five pitch-pine logs every fifteen minutes. It may be readily understood that, since she took about 24 hours to make the trip, little room was available for cargo for some 2,500 logs had to

---

*T. W. GRIFFITH, *Annals of Baltimore*, 1833, p. 248.
†*Niles Register*, Aug. 16, 1817, p. 398.

be stowed at the commencement of each voyage. Not infrequently the steamboats of this period, having been delayed by storm or fog en route, had to finish out their voyages under sail with boilers cold.

Staggering as the wood consumption undoubtedly seems, it must be remembered that at the time a supply of virgin timber considered inexhaustible stood on the banks ready for the axe, and today more trees are felled daily to provide newsprint than all American steamboats of 1820 could consume in weeks.

Benjamin Ferguson owned and independently operated the *Virginia,* the initial voyage over her established route having taken place on August 28, 1817, under the command of Captain John Ferguson. A week prior to that, however, she had been out on an excursion to Havre de Grace and Port Deposit on the Susquehanna. The advertisement read:*

> "This trip is offered to the public for recreation, pleasure and convenience. In passing up the river the novelist will be delighted with the various scenes of nature and art: the ingenuous limmer will find employment for his pencil, the historian for his pen, and the philosopher subjects for contemplation. . ."

Despite these poetic proclivities Captain Ferguson was the logical man to command the *Virginia* for he had been actively connected with Norfolk-Baltimore sailing packets prior to the appearance of the steamboat on the Chesapeake. Although not definitely proven it is said† that Francis Scott Key witnessed on September 13, 1814, the epochal bombardment of Fort McHenry from the deck of "one of Ferguson's Norfolk packets" and was thus inspired to write "The Star Spangled Banner."

Although times of departures were subject to change and delay and, of course, times of arrivals could not be predicted with the clock-work accuracy of today, nevertheless the crude steamboats of this the first decade in their history were an enormous improvement

---

*Baltimore *American,* Aug. 20, 1817, quoted in E. E. LANTZ, *Steamboat on Chesapeake Bay,* Baltimore *Sun,* Jan. 19, 1908.

†By a companion, John Stuart Skinner, who discredited the theory that Key was on the cartel *Analostan.*

over the sailing vessels which they gradually but inevitably began
to replace.

In order to prevent confusion in the use of the term, it would be
well to explain here exactly what differentiated a packet from the
ordinary trading vessel. In former times even though vessels were
advertised to sail on a certain date, if weather was not propitious or
cargo space unfilled, they might stay on in port for days or even
weeks. Later, however, the demand for regular conveyance of passengers and mails brought about the inauguration of packet service.
The vessels so employed advertised their departure for a certain day,
and when it came, sail they did—regardless of weather conditions
or empty cargo holds.

Thus regularized, it is easy to see why packets became popular
for passengers and the better class of freight and also for the transportation of "packets" as the mail was then termed. Fast ships came
into demand for this scheduled service and, when the steamboat
arrived and it began to be possible to predict arrivals with a fair
degree of certainty, the fate of the sailing packet was sealed.

In 1819, the *Virginia* was advertised to leave Newton's Wharf,
Norfolk on Mondays at 9 A. M. and to return leaving Baltimore at
the same hour on Thursdays. The *Virginia* was a fast boat and once
made four passages between Baltimore and Norfolk in as many
days,* although as has been mentioned it was customary for her to
make the round trip in a week. This record trip gave her 86 hours
elapsed time covering a distance of 880 miles, thus making her speed
7.28 knots or 8.5 statute miles an hour. Undoubtedly she was helped
with good winds for without sails her engines were supposed to give
her only 6.4 knots.

Being a novelty, these early steamboats were very popular and
frequently ran summer excursions between their regular runs. One
to Havre de Grace has been mentioned. Another was advertised†
for the *Virginia* in August of 1819 when she was scheduled to leave

---

Niles Register, May 22, 1819, p. 233.
†*American Beacon,* Norfolk, Aug. 6, 1819.

Norfolk "on a party of pleasure to York-Town (Va.) on Saturday next, precisely at seven o'clock in the morning." One must surmise that our ancestors were of a hardier breed, for a 7 A. M. departure would hold scant appeal for trippers today and most certainly could not be categorically classed as an excursion of "pleasure."

Excursion Advertisement—1819 Variety.
From the *American Beacon*, Norfolk, Aug. 3, 1819.

Although hardly pertinent to this work, the late career of the old *Virginia* is not without interest. She served various owners on Chesapeake Bay until in 1845 an announcement was made that "an old Southern passenger packet named *Virginia*" had been purchased and, renamed *Temple of the Muses,* taken to the Hudson River to be rebuilt as a showboat.*

Once begun, the rise of steamboats in the United States was so meteoric as to draw the attention of the world to the progress that was being made. One would like to ascribe full credit for this to American genius alone, but it should be stated that conditions along the Atlantic seaboard and the Western Rivers were most conducive

*Illustrated London News, May 17, 1845, p. 308.

to such development. When first evolved, the steamboat was both unsuitable and unseaworthy for use on the open ocean. America had miles of protected waterways and rivers where the water route was the only one. It is easy to see with their well developed roads on one hand and unprotected coasts on the other, why England and France were slower to adopt the use of steamboats.

This did not cause them to overlook what was going on in America and foreign engineers were sent over by their governments to look into conditions here. One of the most celebrated of these men was the French engineer, Jean Baptiste Marestier, who visited the United States in 1818-1819, and whose invaluable *"Mémoire sur les Bateau à vapeur des États-Unis"* was published in Paris a few years later. American engineers and shipbuilders were too busy to take time out to make drawings and commit their progress to writing and it is significant to note that in many cases the only reliable drawings which have survived came from Marestier's board. Only recently has his rare book come to light and been given its proper recognition. Among other things, his was the only complete plan in existence of the famous *Savannah,* first transatlantic auxiliary steamer.

Marestier's investigations took him to Chesapeake Bay, of course, and without them we should have a very imperfect picture of the first steamboats which plied its waters. The passenger packets he tells us, offered their passengers large saloons carefully ornamented, around the sides of which were placed the double tiers of bunks, *"tenus tres-proprement."*

When the ships were crowded, Marestier remarks that passengers slept on chairs or couches, the dining room tables, or even the floor. Signs requested them to remove their shoes before getting in bed. Ladies had their separate cabin, but came to the men's cabin at mealtime as this also served as dining room. The galley was situated close by the engine room and furnished meals which must have seemed extremely plain to the French palate: at any rate Monsieur Marestier bemoaned the complete lack of *"sauces recherchées,"* and other frills. Vegetables he tells us were boiled in steam drawn from the ship's boiler and the spit was turned by a gear connected with the main paddle shaft. Foreward of the engine room were crews' quarters and storage space.

Several other of the dozen odd steamboats which Marestier counted on the Chesapeake ran from time to time on the Baltimore to Norfolk run. These included the *Roanoke* which ran with the *Virginia* in 1819, the *Surprise,* the *Richmond,* and *Petersburg,* as well as other Baltimore steamboats which made excursions down the Bay.

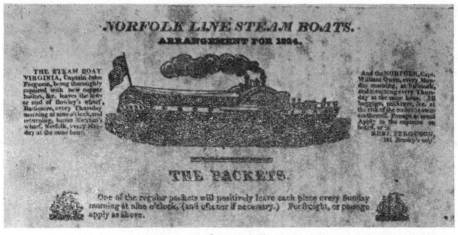

—*Courtesy of The Municipal Museum of the City of Baltimore*

Broadside Advertising Steamship Services in 1824.

The first named, the *Roanoke,* commanded by Captain Middleton, was mostly employed on the James River. She was not a particularly lucky boat and her pair of imported English walking-beam engines gave constant trouble. In 1820 she was put up at auction, but apparently continued running on the James River.

The *Surprise* had the distinction of being propelled by a rotary steam engine, forerunner of the giant turbines used on ocean liners today. George Stiles, a former mayor of Baltimore and owner of privateers in the War of 1812, operated her and she was mainly used between ¡Baltimore, Annapolis, and Easton. Less than a year old, she was badly burned in 1818 at her wharf at a loss of $3,000.

The *Richmond* and the *Petersburg* were essentially James River steamboats. The former made the phenomenal speed of 14 miles an hour on an excursion to City Point in 1819, the year after she was built, and apparently did not come on the Baltimore-Norfolk run until 1830. The "new, swift, and elegant" *Petersburg,* Captain Daniel W. Crocker, was used there at odd times before being cut down to a tow-boat on the Dismal Swamp canal which opened on December 31, 1828.

Following the *Virginia,* however, the next important regular steamboat on the run was the *Norfolk,* which in 1819 cut the scheduled time to twenty hours. The *Norfolk* was almost identical in size to the *Virginia,* but her engine was more powerful and she was equipped with two copper boilers. The *Norfolk* was first owned by the Newbern Steamboat Company and operated on the Carolina Sounds between Elizabeth City and Newbern, N. C., before being sold on April 5, 1820, and taken to Baltimore by Captain John Campbell. Later in the month she was advertised to leave Bowley's Wharf, Baltimore, on Mondays at 9 A. M., returning from Norfolk at the same hour on Fridays.

The year 1828 marks an important turning point in the history of steam navigation on the Chesapeake for during this year a company was formed which absorbed the various individually-owned services competing on the Baltimore-Norfolk run. It was this organization, the Maryland and Virginia Steam Boat Company, which in 1840 was dissolved and reformed as the Baltimore Steam Packet Company.

The Maryland and Virginia Steam Boat Company

CHAPTER III

LITTLE is known of the first years of the Maryland and Virginia Steam Boat Company, nor can it be determined exactly what caused it to wind up its existence after only a dozen years of operation. Probably the financial panic beginning in 1837 largely contributed to its demise. Likewise it should be remembered that during the decade that it spanned a new—at first contributing but later competing—system of transportation came into being—the railroad—of which more will be said anon.

In any event, the new company got off to a good start and began to furnish the public with what was most needed, namely a coördinated system of transportation which tended to eliminate uncertainties and delays. Boats left Baltimore and Norfolk simultaneously and connections for the through traveler were afforded with the Frenchtown packets at one end of the Bay and the James River and Charleston steamboats at the other.

Steamboat travel on the Chesapeake was becoming increasingly reliable and popular and from the handful of craft noted by Marestier ten years before, the registered tonnage had increased in 1827 to 2,207 for Maryland and 946 for Virginia. In order to present a comparative picture it should be stated that Louisiana topped the list with the staggering total of 17,003 tons, with New York following with 10,264 tons.* In both States, the majority of

*Niles Register, July 26, 1828, p. 351.

boats used high-pressure steam boilers and explosions were a common and disastrous occurrence. Conditions became so bad on the Mississippi, that those few vessels which did not use high-pressure steam almost invariably had the words "Low Pressure" painted in large letters across their paddle boxes to reassure prospective travelers. It was stated in 1832 that 14% of all steamers in operation were destroyed by explosions and fires in which approximately a thousand people lost their lives.

On the Hudson River in 1828 a system of "safety trailer" barges had been tried out. The steamboat *Commerce* towed behind it a splendidly appointed barge, the *Lady Clinton,* on which the more fastidious took passage. "Why sleep on the edge of a volcano?" reasonably inquired a contemporary advertisement.* The idea was a good one, but it did not work out for it was impossible to tow the barge at any speed and those whose pocket-books necessitated traveling on the steamboat itself, where rates were less in proportion to the increased risk, did not consider it very sporting.

In juxtaposition to this picture, it should be stated that Chesapeake Bay was remarkably free of steamboat disaster, and proportionately accidents were far less frequent than in other localities. In the meanwhile engineers were designing boilers far better equipped to quietly perform the work they were meant to do, but no type of governmental control existed until 1838, when the U. S. Steamboat Inspection service was founded.

The first vessels owned by the Maryland and Virginia Steam Boat Company were the 1817 *Virginia* and the *Norfolk,* which, as we have already seen, were by this time veterans of the Baltimore-Norfolk line. On September 30, 1828, they were purchased together at auction from the estate of the late Benjamin Ferguson for the sum of $62,500 and at the same time the company contracted with the Baltimore shipbuilding firm of James Beecham and George Gardiner for the construction of two new vessels.

Apparently these two steamboats were built at the same time for

*New York *Enquirer,* June 14, 1828.

they both entered service together in 1829 as the *Columbus* and *Pocahontas.* The latter became in 1840 one of the first boats of the Baltimore Steam Packet Company.

Of the two, the *Columbus* was the larger, measuring 174 feet long by 30 beam and 11 depth. She had the conventional "square" or "cross-head" engine with a single 50-inch cylinder and six-and-a-half-foot stroke, giving her a speed of 10 miles per hour. The *Columbus* ran from Baltimore to Norfolk connecting there with the *Pocahontas* for Richmond. With the other vessels of the line, service was three times weekly and the fare $7 to Norfolk and an additional $3.00 for the trip up the James.

An interesting and slightly hair-raising navigational manœuvre commonly practiced in these times consisted in transferring passengers and cargo from one ship to another out at sea. The celebrated Irish comedian, Tyrone Power, great grandfather of the present moving picture star, has left in his *Impressions of America* a very graphic eye-witness account of these procedures which took place when the steamboat *George Washington* on which he had taken passage from Frenchtown to Baltimore in September, 1834, assisted in such a transfer. Let us have his own words on the subject:*

> Whilst steering through the waters of the Chesapeake, perceived a large steamer standing right for us, with a signal flying. Learned that this was the *Columbus,* bound for Norfolk, Virginia, for which place we had several passengers, who were now to be transhipped to the approaching vessel.
>
> We were out in the open bay, with half a gale of wind blowing, and some sea on; it therefore became a matter of interest to observe how two large ships of this class would approach each other.
>
> The way they managed this ticklish affair was really admirable: before we neared, I observed the Norfolk ship was laid head to wind, and just enough way kept on to steer her; our ship held her course, gradually lessening her speed, until, as she approached the *Columbus,* it barely sufficed to lay and keep her alongside, when they fell together, gangway to gangway: warps were immediately passed, and made secure at both head and stern: and in a minute the huge vessels became as one.
>
> Here was no want of help; the luggage and the passengers were ready at the proper station, so that in a handful of minutes the trans-

---

*T. POWER, *Impressions of America,* 1836, Vol. 2, p. 42-5.

fer was completed without bustle or alarm. Meantime the interest of
this novel scene was greatly increased by the coming up of the inward-
bound Norfolk-man, which flitted close by us amidst the roar occas-
ioned by the escaping steam of the vessels lying-to, a noise that might
have drowned the voice of Niagara.

Posterity is indebted to Mr. Power for being an interested
observer. Here follows a side-light on the kind of passengers which
were southbound on this particular September morning:

> As we thus lay together, I noticed that the upper or promenade deck
> of the *Columbus* was completely taken up by a double row of flashy-
> looking covered carts, or tilt-waggons, as they are called here. Upon
> inquiry, I found that these contained the goods, and were, indeed the
> movable stores, or shops, of that much enduring class, the Yankee
> pedlars, just setting forth for their annual winter cruise amongst the
> plantations of the South: where, however their keen dealing may be
> held in awe, they are looked for with lively anxiety, and their arrival
> greeted as an advent of no little moment. . .
>
> Arranged in a half circle about the bow on the main-deck, I observed
> the horses of these royal pedlars: they stretched their necks out to
> examine us with a keenness of look worthy their knowing masters'
> reputation and their own education.

Apparently the transfer was soon effected. I can imagine no
shipmaster wishing to prolong this delicate manœuvre:

> Our business being completed, the hissing sound of the waste-steam
> pipe ceased, this force being once more applied to its right use; the
> paddles began to move, the lashings were cast off, and away the boats
> darted from each other with startling rapidity: the *Columbus,* with the
> gale aft, rushing down the great bay of the Chesapeake, and the
> *Washington* breasting its force right for Baltimore.

After a few days spent in the "Monumental City," Tyrone Power
continued his southern trip, embarking on the *Columbus* or a sister
ship for Petersburg via Norfolk. "We had a fine day and night whilst
steering through this great bay of the Chesapeake," he wrote. "Went
to bed late in consequence."* He got up early, however, viewed
with interest the partially completed earthworks and moat of Fort
Calhoun (as Fort Monroe was then known), took in the sights of
the Elizabeth River and at 8 A. M. transferred at Norfolk to the

---

*T. POWER, *Impressions of America,* 1836, Vol. 2, p. 72-4.

Pocahontas for City Point while several of his fellow passengers embarked on the *Virginia* for Charleston.

Tyrone Power's century old observations are decidedly refreshing. At a time when numerous foreigners were visiting this country and on their return, penning derogatory remarks about it for their compatriots' edification, Power's "impressions" stand out as being a fair and intelligent appraisal of our young nation and show their author to have been not only an unbiased observer, but also one who managed to enjoy himself in the unfamiliar surroundings and customs he found abroad.

However, we have slighted the memory of one Lieutenant The Hon. Frederick Fitzgerald De Roos, Royal Navy, whose *Personal Narrative of Travels in the United States in 1826* contains the following choice description:*

> The prospect, on entering the Chesapeake Bay, was striking to the greatest degree. The numerous ships, the stillness of the waters, the setting sun shedding its rays on the surrounding beacons, and the rapid course of the steamboat, the ample deck of which was covered with many well-dressed and *some beautiful passengers,* combined to produce a most enchanting effect.

Mr. Power mentioned that on arrival at Norfolk several of his fellow passengers transferred to the *Virginia* for the outside coastal run down to Charleston. The *Virginia,* commanded by Captain William Rollins, had been rebuilt and newly coppered a short time before and included in her alterations was the placing of three masts so that she would be well found under sail alone, for by this time the Bay boats had for the most part dispensed with all auxiliary canvas, except for a single masted rig. Evidently the *Virginia's* ownership passed to the Atlantic Steam Company and in 1835-6 this organization added two new vessels to their Atlantic Line, the *South Carolina* and the *Georgia*[I], 172 feet and 194 feet long respectively, These two vessels came back to Chesapeake Bay shortly before the Baltimore Steam Packet Company was founded.

---

*London, 1827, p. 39-40.

The Maryland and Virginia Steam Boat Company was running the *Pocahontas, Columbus,* and *Norfolk* in 1834 and 1835 and in the latter year they purchased from the People's Steam Navigation Company the *Kentucky,* then the fastest boat on the Bay. The line had not enjoyed an uncontested monopoly of the Baltimore-Norfolk run, however. In 1832 the *Sandusky* had been brought south to offer opposition and she had to be bought off since she could make the trip in only fifteen hours and offered cut rates. In 1835 the *Champion,* Captain Reese, was taken from the Potomac and placed on an opposition line and she too had to be disposed of. The *Kentucky* arranged that, however, for twice she made the run in a little over thirteen hours and her speed killed any permanent or serious opposition by water.

However, the closing years of the Maryland and Virginia Steam Boat Company were marked by stiff opposition from the railroads and to meet this competition they probably overspent themselves in the construction of two brand new boats, the *Jewess* and the *Alabama*[I], of which more will be said anon.

Discounting a stone quarry railroad in New England, the first important road to be chartered in the United States was the Baltimore and Ohio in 1827. This was designed for horse-drawn cars and it was not until half a dozen years later that steam locomotives became important. With the advent of the steam-engine, railroad building increased so rapidly as to become a mania. Unstable land values, defaulted bonds, and other tangible evidences of this sudden growth resulted in the panic of 1837, but this merely proved a hiatus in railroad building and, the depression weathered, the railroads continued spinning their webs of steel rails across the countryside.

At first the rails merely replaced existing stage-coach lines and travelers in 1832 who journeyed from Philadelphia to Baltimore still used two lines of steamers, but crossed the neck of the Eastern Shore Peninsula on the 16-mile Frenchtown-Newcastle railway.

This same year the Portsmouth and Roanoke Railroad was chartered to build a line for almost eighty miles between Portsmouth, Va., and Weldon, N. C. As was to be expected, this line formed a vital feeder to the Norfolk-Baltimore steamboats from the South when, in 1836, the ten-ton engine *Raleigh* hauled its cars over the newly completed line.

The sixth railroad to be chartered in Virginia was the Richmond, Fredericksburg and Potomac, which in 1834 began its line from Richmond northward. Within a few years the rails had been laid to Fredericksburg and a stage line connected with Potomac Creek. Meanwhile Baltimore and Washington had been connected by rails and thus two separate lines were offered the southbound traveler between Baltimore and the Roanoke River in North Carolina. On the one hand these consisted of the already established line of Bay steamers from Baltimore to Norfolk and Portsmouth, whence the rail line extended 77½ miles farther on to Weldon. The other line which became known as the Inland or Upper Route consisted of railroad from Baltimore to Washington, the steamer *Augusta* to Potomac (later Aquia) Creek, stage to Fredericksburg whence the R. F. & P. Railroad continued to Richmond. Continuing south the traveler took the Petersburg Railroad on down to the Roanoke River at Weldon, whence both routes employed the single line which had been built by this time to Wilmington and Charleston.

Some idea of the keenness of the competition between the Bay Line and the Inland route may be gained from the perusal of contemporary advertisements.* No punches were pulled:

> Great Central Route between the North & South via the Chesapeake Bay steamboats and the Portsmouth & Roanoke Rail Road, Oct, 1, 1838: Through from Baltimore to Welston [*sic*], N. C., in twenty-one hours—being four hours in advance of any other Inland Line—without one moment's night travelling on Rail Roads, without loss of sleep, with but one single change of baggage—and at less expense than any other Inland route.

Furthermore, passengers were assured that no "burthen" cars would be attached to their train. The disparagement of competitors was carried to an all-time high in the published statement of the

---

*Petersburg *American Constellation*, Oct. 9, 1838.

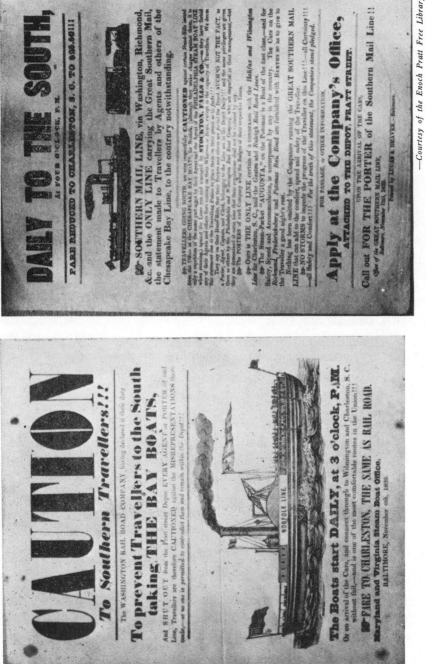

Handbills issued in 1839 by the rival transport lines. Left, Maryland & Virginia Steam Boat Company. Right, the "Upper Route."

Upper Route which advertised in June, 1840, that their passengers reached Charleston one day sooner than those who had taken the Bay steamers and that by their line travelers would "avoid being compelled to remain ALL NIGHT AT WELDON, on the Roanoke,—one of the most UNHEALTHY PLACES in the Southern Country, where by the Bay Line, they are delayed SEVENTEEN HOURS."*

It is not beyond a great stretch of the imagination to assume that on reading this the inhabitants of Weldon bent every effort to divert north-bound travelers away from the Upper Route. Baltimore, however, felt the keenest competition and both lines had their agents and "runners" stationed to meet passengers arriving from Philadelphia to shower them with handbills. Two of these, one issued by each line, are reproduced as illustrations, therefore need not be quoted.

Although mention of it here anticipates a chronological recounting of events, it should be stated that when the Baltimore Steam Packet Company came into being it inherited the rivalry developed by the Maryland and Virginia Steam Boat Company and the very first advertisement placed by the new company squared away with the statement that:†

> The public are therefore cautioned to put no trust in the malicious falsehoods circulated by the Agents of the Upper Route against this Line (they keep out of view their own mishaps and deficiencies), but may rely on the Statements made by the above Line.

Through the early period of their existence they continued to lose no opportunity of reminding prospective travelers of the Upper Route's peccadillos, viz.:‡

> For 25 years there has been a line of steamboats to Norfolk and yet there never has been an accident—therefore the croakings about "Fogs," "Rough Weather," "Storms," "Risks," "boats urged to the top of their speed," &c. are altogether the humbugs of a fruitful imagination, gotten up to impose upon the credulous. The Baltimore Steam Packet Company and the Portsmouth and Roanoke Rail Road Company hereby pledge themselves that the connection by their route is perfect.

---

*Baltimore *American*, June 20, 1840.
†Baltimore *American*, Sept. 12, 1840.
‡Baltimore *American*, Dec. 18, 1840.

It is amusing to note that while the Upper Route shuddered at the dangers attendant to a lengthy visit to Weldon, the Bay Line advertised that at this place their passengers could enjoy a "comfortable rest."

We must assume that due to the natural skepticism and confusion which it produced, muck-raking did little good to encourage prospective travelers to use either line. In any event there was business enough for both and the caliber of later advertising copy was noticeably toned down.

The year 1838 was an important one in the history of steam navigation not only on the Chesapeake but in the world at large. The arrival at New York on April 22 of the two British steamers *Sirius* and *Great Western* within a few hours of each other focused nation-wide attention on the successful use of ocean steamers. Unlike previous Atlantic crossings, these two passages had been for the most part under steam alone and the fact that sufficient fuel could be carried for the entire trip across the ocean was demonstrated.

The town of Baltimore had also welcomed a transatlantic steamer when the British auxiliary bark *City of Kingston* arrived at the head of the Chesapeake from the West Indies and sailed thence for London direct on May 20. Like the famous *Savannah* of two decades prior, the *City of Kingston* was essentially a sailing vessel, but Baltimorians were nevertheless wildly excited at the prospect of establishing direct steam communication with Europe.

Upon this rosy picture, the disaster to the steam-packet *Pulaski* fell like a bomb-shell. Over a hundred lives were lost when this Baltimore-Charleston boat exploded her boiler off Cape Hatteras on June 14. People well remembered that only the year before the New York-Charleston packet *Home* had fared a similar fate when her back was broken in a storm off Hatteras' raging seas. Naturally the business of the Atlantic Line from Norfolk to Charleston in which the Maryland and Virginia Steam Boat Company was interested suffered enormously and probably added another coffin nail to the troubles it was experiencing as a result of over-expansion plus cut-rate competition from the Inland Route.

We have mentioned that the Maryland and Virginia Steam Boat Company had built two steamboats shortly before it terminated operations. The largest of these, the *Alabama*[I], was essentially a coastwise rather than a sound steamer and had probably been built for a run similar to that of the ill-fated *Pulaski*. This ocean route was abandoned shortly thereafter with the result that although she was undoubtedly a fine vessel, the *Alabama* turned out to be too big for her times on Chesapeake Bay.

When completed she was described in a contemporary account as being "without exception the most splendid steam boat that ever floated on the waters of the Chesapeake."* Levin H. Dunkin of Baltimore was the builder and her 200 horse-power engine installed by Messrs. Charles Reeder and Sons gave her a cruising speed of fifteen miles an hour. Like her predecessors, the *Alabama* was a side-wheeler with wooden hull, coppered and copper-fastened, and cost $107,000 to build: exactly twice the amount of the *Virginia* which had been hailed as the epitome of the steamboat builder's art twenty years before.

The *Alabama's* interior accommodations (she was "carpeted throughout with the best of Brussels") consisted of: main saloon, 54 berths; ladies' cabin, 32 berths; forward cabin, 40 berths; and in addition she had four staterooms on deck. This early mention of staterooms on Chesapeake Bay craft is not without interest, but considerable time was still to elapse before staterooms on sound steamers became the rule rather than a "de luxe" exception.

The *Alabama* was rigged with three masts as was the custom on ocean-going steamboats and she measured 210 feet in length and 676 tons "burthen."

The second vessel built for the Maryland and Virginia Steam Boat Company during the year 1838 proved more suitable for the trade and was one of the vessels with which the Baltimore Steam

---

*Baltimore *American*, Sept. 19, 1840.

Packet Company began service in 1840. This vessel was christened *Jewess* and her 173½-foot length is said to have terminated in an imposing gilded eagle figure-head. Her lever-beam engine by Wells, Miller and Clark gave her a speed of 14 miles per hour and she could carry seventy-five passengers "comfortably."

Undoubtedly some of its older boats had been sold when the *Alabama* and *Jewess* were added to the Maryland and Virginia Steam Boat Company fleet, for in the wind-up of affairs in 1840 these two vessels plus only the *Pocahontas* and *Columbus* were offered "including all their tackle, apparel and furniture" at public auction at the Merchants' Exchange in Baltimore.*

*Baltimore *American,* Sept. 19, 1840.

The Baltimore Steam Packet Company
Makes Its Bow

CHAPTER IV

AT the December session of the General Assembly of Maryland in 1839, "An Act to Incorporate the Baltimore Steam Packet Company" was passed. The preamble of Section I stated:

Be it enacted by the General Assembly of Maryland, That William McDonald, Robert A. Taylor, Joel Vickers, John S. McKim, John B. Howell, Benjamin Buck, Samuel McDonald, Thomas Kelso, Andrew F. Henderson and others, their successors and assigns, be and are hereby, created and made a corporate and body politic, by the name and title of the BALTIMORE STEAM PACKET COMPANY,—and by that name and title shall have perpetual succession, . . . and generally [are authorized] to do all such acts as shall be proper and necessary for the purpose of employing one or more steamboats to navigate the Chesapeake Bay and its tributary streams, or to navigate the Atlantic Coast, or any of the bays or rivers emptying into the Atlantic Ocean—and to connect thereto boats, vessels, stages or other carriages, for the conveyance of passengers, towing of ships, vessels, rafts or arks, and the transportation of merchandise or other articles.

This Charter then, with the exception of certain amendments added through the years, has remained for a century the basis of the Old Bay Line's activities, even though they have never taken advantage of the authorization to tow any "arks." The "other carriages" mentioned undoubtedly refer to railroads.

We have seen that Andrew F. Henderson, who became the Old Bay Line's first president, and General William McDonald had both been associated with Chesapeake steamboating since its beginnings back in 1813. Others of the incorporators were particularly ship-minded men, John S. McKim being owner of the famous Baltimore clipper *Ann McKim.*

The new steam packet company's first general agent was John C. Moale who had been president of the Maryland and Virginia Steam

"View of Baltimore, Maryland, from Federal Hill." The *Alabama,* 1838, appears in t left center of the print alongside her wharf. The Old Bay Line steamers *Georgia, Jewe.*

Boat Company and trustee when it went into liquidation and disposed of its fleet. Thomas Sheppard, was appointed treasurer and he too had previously been associated with steamboat operation, having served in the same office for the Atlantic Line.

—*Courtesy The Municipal Museum of the City of Baltimore.*

and *Herald* may be identified elsewhere. (After the lithograph by E. Whitefield, New York, 1847.)

—Courtesy of National Maritime Museum, England.

The little wooden side-wheeler *Pocahontas* built at Baltimore in 1829 for the Maryland &
Virginia Steam Boat Company became in 1840 one of the first ships of the Old Bay Line.
(From a contemporary drawing.)

In acquiring several of the Maryland and Virginia Steam Boat
Company's ships, the new line likewise fell heir to some of their
captains: James Coffey, Thomas Sutton, James Cannon, G. W.
Russell, and James Holmes. Apparently Captain William Rollins,
who had served as master of both the *Virginia* and the *Georgia*[I]
on the Charleston run and was alleged to have been the new company's first commander, did not remain long in its employ, for a
short time afterwards he is mentioned as master of the New Orleans-
Havana steam packet *Neptune* and later of the *Isabel*.

When the boats with which the Baltimore Steam Packet Company began operation were purchased second-hand from the Atlantic
Line and the Maryland and Virginia Steam Boat Company, the
oldest and smallest was the *Pocahontas,* built in 1829. A contemporary drawing which has turned up in a British collection shows

her to have been a tubby little craft with two tall smoke-stacks rising up from boilers placed out over the guards, an arrangement designed to insure less damage to the boat itself if at any time the boilers elected to explode.

Next in point of age was the comparatively new steamer *South Carolina* launched in 1835 and which, as stated, was operated by the Atlantic Line to Charleston. The description of her which appeared in the newspapers prior to her sale at auction reported that she was 172 feet long and had been recently "repaired, caulked, newly coppered, and logged; . . . has the best inventory, and is well calculated for 150 to 200 passengers, has about 150 life preservers. . ."*

The reader's attention is called to the fact that her owners quite nonchalantly advertised her capacity at 200 passengers with "about" 150 life preservers. Some years were still to elapse before it became obligatory to reverse this ratio and then there was nothing indefinite permitted about the number of life-preservers provided.

The *Georgia*[I], also built for the Atlantic Line in 1836, has already been described in connection with our "Mr. Smith's" voyage a century ago, and it was at this time that the Baltimore Steam Packet Company also acquired the 1838 *Jewess* from the former Norfolk-Baltimore line.

There is some question as to whether the new line actually took title to the *Alabama*[I]. In any event she was not purchased along with the other Maryland and Virginia Steam Boat Company ships and although mention is made in the reports of the directors of the appointment of Mr. A. G. Ramsey as engineer, the *Alabama* was evidently held as a spare boat and not used on the regular run. It was not long after the company commenced business that she was scheduled to quit Baltimore for good, running down to New Orleans to be put into service as a Havana packet.

The Maryland and Virginia Steam Boat Company ships had been maintaining a daily schedule leaving Baltimore in the mid-afternoon. In its second published advertisement the Baltimore

---

*Baltimore *American*, Sept. 19, 1840.

Steam Packet Company "informed" the public that it would maintain the same service. Shortly thereafter, the time of departure from Spears Wharf, Baltimore, was advanced to 9. A. M. with arrival at Portsmouth at 11 P. M., but when winter came on the schedule was abbreviated to tri-weekly and the boats again ran over-night, leaving Baltimore on Tuesdays, Thursdays and Sundays. The fare to Norfolk was $8, meals included.

However, the tri-weekly service called for sailings falling on Sundays and not long after, the daily schedule was again adopted and a resolution of the Board of Directors carried on February 23, 1841, stated that:

> This board are desireous to avoid the violation of the Sabbath by causing their boats to be employed on that day. Therefore, the Agent is instructed to communicate with the President of the Portsmouth and Roanoke Rail Road, informing him that as soon as the *Jewess* can be gotten ready for this company, we will start a line of boats from each end of the line daily, Sundays excepted, until further notice.

The following other manifestations of Company policy as reflected by the deliberations of the board are not without an element of humor:

> Whereas this board has observed the pleasure and great progress now making in the temperance cause, and believing (nay they know) that there is too much ardent spirits consumed by persons in the employ of this Company, therefore be it resolved that the Captains, Clerks, Mates and all others . . . are hereby earnestly requested to abstain altogether in the use of intoxicating drinks. . .

This was all very well as far as the employees of the Line were concerned, but for the passengers it was another matter. All the boats had well patronized bars, lucrative concessions of the captains, the profits from which were not to be ignored. At the same meeting:

> Letters were read from Mr. Wilson, Clerk of the *Georgia* and Mr. Aspirl, Clerk of the *Alabama,* asking the Board to allow them to participate in the profits of the Bar jointly with the Captain. On motion duly seconded, the Board ordered the profits or losses of the Bar to be divided equally between the Captains and Clerks until further action of the Board.

Business was good for the first year of the Company's existence and opposition by the steamboat *Boston* ("having the newly invented safety valves") did not last long and Captain James Holmes, who had formerly been with the Bay Line in command of the *Jewess,* transferred the *Boston* to the Norfolk-Washington run with more success.

However, the wooden steamboats of a century ago were not long-lived and on September 7, 1841, the company signed a contract for their first new ship with the Baltimore builders of Brown and Collyer. This specified the construction of an 180-foot steamer with a lever-beam engine and boilers of the "best Pennsylvania iron."

This vessel proved to be the ill-fated *Medora* which blew up on her trial trip. Perhaps a revengeful fate had read the advertisement which stated that there had been no accidents on the line for twenty-five years. It would be well to quote here from a contemporary account of the disaster which absolved the Bay Line as follows:*

> It should be borne in mind that the steamboat *Medora,* at the time of the accident, was yet in the hands of the builders, she having never been delivered to the Baltimore and Norfolk Steam-packet Company, for whose use she was built. No accident of the kind has ever happened to any boat while under the control of the careful agents of this Company.

Apparently this sentiment was generally entertained by the traveling public. In any event the line did not suffer from lack of confidence, and still having the need for an additional steamer, as soon as the debris could be cleared, work went forward to reclaim what was left of the *Medora* to be applied to the construction of another vessel.

However, the disaster was one of the most appalling ever to have taken place on the Chesapeake. On the afternoon of April 14, 1842, the newly completed *Medora* preparatory to embarking on her trial trip was lying at the wharf of her engine builder, John Watchman, on the south side of the Basin. Numerous officials of the line and their invited guests were on board which, with shipyard workers

---

*Baltimore *American,* April 16, 1842.

and her regular crew, brought the total number of persons up to seventy-nine. At the second revolution of her paddles as she backed away from the dock, the boiler exploded without warning carrying up with it a considerable portion of the upper deck and those on it and blowing the smoke-stack high into the air. The main force of the explosion was almost exclusively towards the bow and the boiler itself, an "immense one of iron," was hurled upwards and landed crosswise on the deck. Clouds of scalding steam instantly enveloped the ill-fated craft and many persons who escaped the explosion were carried down with her as she sank.

According to the historian, Colonel J. T. Scharf:[*]

> The scene presented by the boat afforded at once a mournful evidence of the immense power of steam, and of the ruin of which it can be the instrument. Large oak beams were splintered to pieces; iron bars that would have withstood the strength of a hundred men, were broken and wrenched into many shapes; the lighter wood-work of the deck was blown almost to atoms.

A pall of gloom immediately settled over the town as rescue workers answering the immediate plea of Mayor Soloman Hillen started out on their gruesome mission of recovering the dead. At intervals during the day a cannon was fired over the water on the assumption that the concussion would cause sunken bodies to rise to the surface.

At the final tabulation 26 persons were dead and 38 injured, but 15 escaping. A serious blow to the new company was suffered in the deaths of its president, Andrew F. Henderson, and its general agent, John C. Moale, who was struck down along with one of his two sons. Captain Sutton commanding the *Medora* was thought to be fatally injured, but the hardy mariner survived to pilot many a subsequent Old Bay Line ship. Captain Coffey of the *Georgia* was also injured, fortunately only slightly.

Contemporary newspapers made the most of the event in a ghoulish manner, one containing a hurriedly executed woodcut of

---

[*] J. T. Scharf, *Chronicles of Baltimore*, 1874, p. 505-6.

—*Courtesy The Mariners' Museum.*

"Views of Norfolk and Portsmouth from the Marine Hospital." The steamboat *Herald* (1842) is shown leaving port in the left center of the print. Note the livestock on the fore deck. Lower inset views are of Old Point and the Gosport Navy Yard. (After the lithograph by E. Sachse, Baltimore, 1851.)

the gruesome scene with bodies flying in all directions.* Others gave hair-raising accounts of various incidents which must have made ghastly reading for the survivors.

Naturally an investigation was made into the cause of the explosion, but it was impossible to ascribe blame with certainty either to the engineers or the builders.† Strangely enough, although apparently trivial matters such as the bar profits were mentioned in the reports of the directors, no comment on the *Medora* disaster occurs in their annual minute books. Perhaps at the time the event seemed too bitterly close home to warrant any mention of it at all.

Robert A. Taylor succeeded Mr. Henderson as president and service with the old boats, the *Georgia,* Captain Coffey, and the *Jewess,* Captain Russell, continued without interruption. Even an excursion was advertised the next month in connection with the Volunteer Military Encampment at Baltimore on May 16, "passage and fare" for the round trip from Norfolk being set at $5.00 for those "disposed to take the trip."

Meanwhile, work on rebuilding the *Medora* continued and before the end of the year the new steamer christened *Herald,* was added to the line and became its first expressly constructed ship. If the *Medora's* career was short and disastrous, rebuilt as the *Herald,* she enjoyed a remarkably long and useful life. She ran on Chesapeake Bay until after the War of Secession and was then taken to the Hudson River and used as a tug. Finally, in her forty-third year, she was dropped from the *List of Merchant Vessels* as "abandoned" on September 30, 1885.

In the meanwhile she had received at least two new boilers and had been practically rebuilt when lengthened from 184 feet to 215 feet in 1849. Captain George W. Russell was appointed master when she came out on October 21, 1842, and James Cannon, who had previously commanded Bay Line ships, was first mate.

Competition with the Upper Route continued to be keen and

Dixon's Letter, New York, April 14, 1842.
†*Niles Register,* April 23, 1842, p. 128.

when the R. F. & P. Railroad extended its line from Fredericksburg to Aquia Creek on the Potomac, eliminating an uncomfortable stagecoach route, the schedule of the railroad was advanced with proportionate inducement to the traveler. It will be remembered that when Charles Dickens visited America early in 1842, he traveled over this route on his way from Washington to Richmond and thus left a memorable picture not only of his steamboat trip down the Potomac, but also of the discomforts of stage travel. The great novelist had planned to return from Richmond via the James River and the Bay Line, but, "one of the steam-boats being absent from her station through some accident, and the means of conveyance being consequently rendered uncertain,"* he returned to Washington by the way he had come. Thus, by this narrow margin the Old Bay Line missed being immortalized in his writings. However, his *American Notes* do not always speak too highly of what their author found on this side of the Atlantic, even though he did praise Barnum's Hotel in Baltimore because he had not only curtains to his bed, but also "enough water for washing." Later in his tour he embarked on the steamboat *Burlington* on Lake Champlain, and here, too, he penned pæans of praise in behalf of a steamboat "superior . . . to any other in the world. This steamboat . . . is a perfectly exquisite achievement of neatness, elegance, and order. The decks are drawing-rooms; the cabins are boudoirs. . ."†

As a result of the competing service, masters and engineers of Bay Line steamers were "strictly enjoined that they do not make their trips between Baltimore and Norfolk in less than 15 hours" even though the boats were not to be driven too hard with resultant "ware and tare" on the machinery. In 1842, with the *Herald* in operation, the regular Bay Line steamers left Baltimore on Mondays, Wednesdays, Fridays, and Saturdays at 4 P. M. and the *Pocahontas* sailed once a week from Baltimore direct to Petersburg and Richmond. The former rival steamboat *Boston* was again on the route and, her

*CHARLES DICKENS, *American Notes*, 1842, Vol. 2, p. 24.
†*Ibid.*, p. 208-9.

—*Courtesy of Maryland Historical Society.*

Old Bay Line Advertisement from a Baltimore Directory of 1845.

owners not possessing the same sentiments about desecrating the Sabbath, she ran on Sundays and Thursdays.

In 1845, an affiliated steamboat company was founded expressly for navigating the James River. This, the Powhatan Line, running ships from Baltimore to Richmond, acquired the venerable *Pocahontas* from the Bay Line, and also the old *Columbus* on which Tyrone Power had taken passage in the days of the Maryland and Virginia Steam Boat Company.

The Bay Line's difficulties in attracting through travelers increased with the abandonment of the Portsmouth and Roanoke Railroad's service south to Weldon in April of the same year or as its President and Directors put it, "the cars ceased to run." This gave the Upper route the more direct line, for now through-passengers on the Bay boats had to be routed on up the James and Appomattox Rivers to Petersburg to catch the railroad thence to Weldon which formerly had competed with the Portsmouth and Roanoke.

Naturally this increased the importance of the Baltimore Steam Packet Company's James River link and in October of that year they acquired an 11/32 interest in the side-wheeler *Alice,* and ran her from Norfolk to City Point. Soon after, the Richmond and Petersburg Railroad organized their own line of boats on the James and the Bay Line retaliated by purchasing another vessel, the iron-hulled *Mount Vernon,* to place on the Appomattox. This condition was alleviated in 1851 when a reorganized Seaboard and Roanoke Railroad took over the abandoned tracks between Portsmouth and Weldon and replaced the old wooden rails with the latest iron "T" rails. The Baltimore Steam Packet Company to whom this southern feeder had been so vital, immediately bought a majority of the stock of the new railroad company to see to it that it would keep going.*

Meanwhile, however, the R. F. & P. succeeded in purchasing a controlling interest in the Bay Line—Seaboard and Roanoke combine, and the two systems, bitter rivals since the days of the Maryland

*T. J. WERTENBAKER, *Norfolk—Historic Southern Port,* 1931, p. 197.

and Virginia Steam Boat Company, fell for the time under one control.

In this year (1851), Virginia had some 74 steamboats in commission, an increase of 700% over the number licensed in this State twenty years before.* Travel by boat had been slowly and surely gaining in popularity and during the period up until the War of Secession, many important steam-boat lines were established. Perhaps the most important of these was the celebrated Fall River Line of Long Island Sound, which began in 1847 and whose lamented termination occurred only a short time ago in its ninety-first year of operation. The famous Fall River was destined to become the standard sound transportation line in the world and the record of its long existence is studded with interest and glamour.† In 1852, another famous old line came into being, the Merchants and Miners Transportation Company, which has expanded its initial service from Baltimore to Providence to cover today numerous routes along the Atlantic coast.‡

Things went along fairly smoothly during the first decade of the company's history. The service averaged tri-weekly in Winter and daily in Summer, at which time extra boats of the line were employed, whenever possible, running excursions. Usually the latter proved to be well ordered affairs, but on one occasion events took place that proved considerably embarrassing to the steamship owners.

Colonel J. T. Scharf mentions in his *Chronicles of Baltimore* that:§

> On the 5th of July [1847] an alarming riot took place between the citizens of Annapolis and a portion of the passengers of the steamer *Jewess*. The steamer left Baltimore on an excursion to St. Michael's; when about twenty miles down the river it was found that in consequence of the crowded state of the boat, it would be dangerous to cross the bay to the Eastern Shore, and accordingly, after consultation, it was determined to run into Annapolis. After a short time a fight was started on the wharf between some citizens of the town and some of

---

*DeBows Commercial Review, 1852, p. 309.
†See R. W. McAdam, The Old Fall River Line, 1937.
‡See Tales of the Coast (Merchants & Miners), 1927.
§Pages 524-5.

the young men who were on the boat. In a few minutes the fight became general, and for the time assumed a fearful character. Stones, bricks, and missils in abundance were thrown indiscriminately upon the boat, striking ladies and children as well as others.

Shortly after, some of the passengers got hold of rifles and fired on the Annapolis crowd, injuring five people. The citizens retaliated by procuring two small cannon which they dragged over to the common by the wharf and were preparing to fire on the *Jewess* when (and about time too) she shoved off for the return to Baltimore.

Another noteworthy event of its early years is recorded in an extract from a company resolution dated December 21, 1846, and preserved in the annual volumes of minutes of the directors. It stated:

> RESOLVED, That the brave and meritorious conduct of Mr. Geo. S. Moore, Second Mate of the Steamer *Georgia,* Capt. Russell, on her trip from Baltimore to Norfolk, and those worthy men who accompanied him in the arduous and dangerous exploit by venturing in the small boat of the *Georgia* while crossing the Horse Shoe in that dreadful gale and snow storm of the morning of the 17 December, 1846, the sea running mountains high, to save a fellow mortal, one of the crew of said steamboat who was knocked overboard by the Chain Roc [chain plate (?)] giving way, from a watery grave, and with great exertion saved the unfortunate man. For this humane act, the Board express their warmest praise and for the injury received by Mr. Moore in having his hand much lacerated and mashed, they in order that he may apply the proper advice and remedies for restoring the same to a healthy condition, they make him a present of twenty dollars.
>
> * * * *
>
> The Committee also in order to alleviate the suffering of the poor colored man, Westley Banks, who was extricated from this awful death in being knocked overboard on 17 December 1846 in that dreadful snow storm and gale from which he received some injury, present him with five dollars.

It may perhaps detract slightly from the anti-climax we experience on learning of the munificence of the awards to point out that in those days a dollar was really worthy of the name and actually the company was acting without precedent in making any contribution at all.

In 1848, Moor N. Falls succeeded Robert A. Taylor as president of the Line. Although it had only been going for eight years and had had one brand new boat added in 1842, the need for expansion was again felt. We have mentioned that the *Herald* had been lengthened in 1849. During a waterfront fire, all too common in those days, the *Jewess* together with the *Governor Walcott* and two schooners had been badly burned at their wharfs on January 11, 1848. The *Jewess* was about to start south when the accident occurred, and although the "Great Southern Mail" was saved, most of the upper works and her cargo was destroyed. She was rebuilt by Flannegan & Trimble and lengthened from 173½ feet to 199 feet in the process.

This gave the line in the year 1851 the *Georgia* and *Herald* for over-night Winter service, and the *Jewess* joined them in the daily schedule of the Summer months at which time the boats made their runs in daylight. As the railroad was again in operation from Portsmouth, the importance of the James River service was diminished and the company had disposed of their little river steamers *Alice* and *Mount Vernon*. The former was taken to New London, Conn., but the latter continued to run on the James and the regular Bay Line ships connected with the Powhatan Line which was operating the *Mount Vernon* and the *Curtis Peck* for Richmond and Petersburg, and a separate line which ran the *Star* to Suffolk. It may be assumed that by this time the little *Pocahontas* was completely worn out and had been left to fall to pieces.

It was obvious to the company officials that with the various advances made in the development of steamboats in the decade that they had been in existence, that their boats had been rendered obsolete and in order to keep in business that they would have to supply an increasingly more discriminating public with new and larger ships. On Long Island Sound the Norwich Line steamer *Atlantic* had come out in 1846, the first sound steamboat to use illuminating gas. Although until the advent of electricity in the 1880's, the danger of fire on this account was ever present, still piped illuminating gas on shipboard was a considerable improvement over the feeble kerosene lamps, spitting candles, and whale-oil tapers that it replaced.

Engines and boilers had likewise seen remarkable changes both in increased power and safety. Passengers were now no longer satisfied with the more or less public dormatories which characterized the accommodation of early steamboats, and demanded private cabins.

Chesapeake Bay Steamboat *Louisiana.* The *Louisiana* built by Cooper and Butler in 1854 was the largest of the Old Bay Line's wooden hull passenger steamers. Note the "Hog Frame." (After a contemporary lithograph.)

A Pair of "Superb and Commodious" Steamboats

CHAPTER V

AKING all these advances into consideration a building committee was appointed which reported to the Bay Line directors on June 17, 1851, that they had received estimates from five shipbuilding firms in Baltimore and Philadelphia for the construction of a 235-foot steamboat, of 31½ feet in beam and 11-foot hold. It is interesting to note that in those days, the owners themselves selected the various sub-contractors for the construction of machinery, joiner work, painting, and furnishings. Today, of course, in practically all cases the shipyard estimates on the whole job and does not merely expect to furnish a bare hull.

For comparison with present-day prices, here are some of the estimates of the various successful bidders as broken down for the wooden side-wheel steamer under consideration. This vessel entered the Bay Line the following year as the *North Carolina:*

> To Cooper & Butler, $20,000 for the hull of the boat at $25. per ton.
>
> To Murray & Hazlehurst, $29,200 for a vertical beam engine, 56 inches in diameter by 11-foot stroke and two tubular boilers, "suited to the use of wood or coal," plus installation.
>
> To Charles & Geo. W. Morris, $10,000 for joiner work, "including the gilding."
>
> To Walter Ball, $2,500 for painting.
>
> To S. Beacham, 7½ cents per pound for iron work.

The committee concluded its report with the statement that the "probable cost of the new steamboat may be, including suitable and appropriate furniture, somewhat upwards of $70,000."

It was upwards. On the books the value of the *North Carolina* stood at $111,272.03. However, in the end they got a better equipped and slightly larger ship, for, as completed, their new steamboat measured 239.3 x 33.5 x 11.2 and had an engine of 60-inch cylinder diameter.

Despite the increased cost, the *North Carolina* proved so satisfactory from the first that the company decided to put the *Jewess* up for sale and to build a new running mate. The various proposals for the construction of this second new steamer were carried out in similar manner, Cooper & Butler again furnishing the hull, but Charles Reeder & Sons, the engine. On May 1, 1854, the building committee mentioned their,

> . . . regret to conclude this report by announcing their great disappointment in not having it in their power to inform you of the boat having been launched, which has been through no fault of theirs.

A week later they stated that,

> The *Louisiana* is doubtless one of the most substantial, commodious, and elegant boats of the day, but exceeding in expenditure of money the sum which our former views indicated.

From the contemporary views of her that have survived, we can agree that the *Louisiana* did represent about the best then technologically possible. Her hull was of tough white oak and cedar wood, copper and iron fastened and painted white above the waterline as was customary. She carried the characteristic "hog bracing frame" typical of all wooden hulled sound steamers. This consisted of a pair of heavy wood bridge trusses which ran parallel to each other for the greater part of the length of the boat. These gave rigidity and stiffness to a shallow draft hull which might otherwise sag at the ends or become "hogged" when the weight of cargo did not evenly balance the concentrated weight of the machinery amidships.

The *Louisiana* measured exactly 266 feet, 2½ inches in length, and she was not only one of the largest boats on Chesapeake Bay, but also she remained the largest wooden-hulled craft ever operated by the Old Bay Line. Her maiden voyage commanded by Capt. Russell took place on November 9, 1854, and on an excursion to Old Point Comfort and the Virginia Capes which took place on the following day, the captain's Norfolk and Portsmouth friends presented him with a "magnificient silver speaking trumpet."* Although by this time a system of bells had been evolved to communicate signals from pilot house to engine room, nevertheless captains still gave most of their orders verbally and one can well imagine that feminine hearts palpitated at the sight of this fine seaman brandishing his gleaming trumpet from his station on top of one of the paddle boxes.

The acquisition of its two splendid new and modern steamboats raised the Old Bay Line to a class second to none, and inspired the Norfolk historian, William S. Forrest, to write that:†

> This line is so well and ably conducted, that accidents seldom or never happen. The boats are very superior, kept in the finest order, and are in charge of officers of long experience, and well-tried skill and judgment.

With the *Louisiana* joining the *North Carolina* on the run it was possible to maintain an eleven-hour schedule. Thus, two boats leaving port simultaneously were all that were needed for daily service.

Meanwhile travelers' written opinions of the line varied between highest praise and severest condemnation. Suffice it to say, the passenger business picked up so much that even the large new boats were often crowded. One choloric passenger en route to the Balti more Fair in 1855 was forced to seek repose on the deck of the main cabin, where he complained that "the heat was fearful, but odours of tobacco juice and liquors were worse." On arrival, however, he confessed that the steamer had made "great progress."‡

Still another voyager on Chesapeake Bay steamboats described them§ as "elegantly carpeted and furnished; frequently with most profuse gilding, mirrors, ottomans, etc." He mentioned that the dining saloon was below the main deck and although smoking was not allowed in the "grand saloons," passengers might employ the

*H. W. BURTON, *History of Norfolk*, 1877, p. 19.
†W. S. FORREST, *Historical Sketches of Norfolk and Vicinity*, 1853, p. 155.
‡C. R. WELD, *A Vacation Tour of the U. S. and Canada*, 1855, p. 330.
§J. W. HENGISTON, *Something of Baltimore, Washington, the Chesapeake and Potomac*, in Colburn's *New Monthly Magazine*, London, 1853, p. 358-373.

weed on the "piazza." Both shower and "plunge" baths were advertised.

The year 1855 has been described as one "that will never be forgotten in Norfolk."* During the summer a case of yellow fever was discovered on board the ocean steamer *Benjamin Franklin* and almost overnight the disease spread rapidly throughout Portsmouth and then Norfolk. Events of those critical times when people were dropping "like withered leaves shaken by the winds" are graphically described in contemporary accounts which read like Defoe's *Journal of the Plague Year in London* [1666]. Suffice it to say, the Old Bay Line rendered invaluable assistance in evacuating refugees and carrying "the necessaries of life for the relief of the sufferers" freight free.

On January 2, 1856, the Maryland General Assembly extended the charter of the Baltimore Steam Packet Company to run another twenty years and later also passed an amendatory act authorizing the company "to make contracts for breaking tracks through the ice." Apparently the winter of this year was a very severe one and for several weeks all shipping was frozen in, unable to move. At this time the *Georgia*[I] was said to have been "much damaged" but no particulars have survived.† The same year employees of the company purchased "a set of silver as a present to M. N. Falls, Esq., the popular president."‡

Reproduced as an illustration is a facsimile of a broadside advertisement issued in September, 1858. By this time the rebuilt railroad lines running south from Portsmouth were in good order and agreements with this and other rail lines made it possible for the Baltimore Steam Packet Company to offer through tickets from New York to Wilmington, N. C. With the faster steamers ("replete with every comfort and convenience") in operation, departure from

---

*T. J. WERTENBAKER, *Norfolk—Historic Southern Port,* 1931, p. 210-216. See also H. W. BURTON, *History of Norfolk,* 1877, p. 19-24.
†*Nautical Magazine,* April 1856, p. 63.
‡H. W. BURTON, *History of Norfolk,* 1877, p. 24.

—*Courtesy of Mr. L. R. Powell, Jr.*

Old Bay Line Advertisement of 1858.

Baltimore was put off from four until five P. M. Tickets, Baltimore
to Norfolk, had been reduced to $5.00.

In 1859, the line suffered its second major castastrophe in the
destruction by fire of the *North Carolina,* then less than five and a
half years old. Fortunately few passengers (only 26 all told) were
aboard when, early in the morning of January 30, a fire started in
one of the upper staterooms and almost instantaneously ignited the
whole steamboat. Two persons were lost, a passenger, the Rev. Mr.
Curtis, and a colored steward, Isaac Watters.

"Harry Scratch," the Norfolk newspaperman, mentioned* that
"seven ladies barely escaped in their night clothes," and we may
assume that this may be taken literally as well as figuratively. Apparently the heroes of the occasion were Captain Cannon, master of
the ship, and a passenger, Captain Henry Fitzgerald, who jumped
out of his lifeboat several times to rescue women and children. A
Mr. William Denby, Jr., was also "highly complimented for his
coolness and presence of mind in that trying time."

When passengers and crew were safely in the lifeboats, they
rowed over to Smith's Point light-ship where they remained until
the steamer *Locust Point* picked them all up and carried them down
to Old Point Comfort. Ship and cargo were a total loss and most
of the passengers escaped with only their lives. Occasions like this
call for an almost superhuman display of seamanship and the prompt
action of Captain Cannon and his crew undoubtedly prevented the
disaster to the *North Carolina* from becoming an appalling tragedy
similar to the comparatively recent holocaust of the *Morro Castle.*

Although obviously the *North Carolina* was badly burned before
she sank, nevertheless it was considered possible to salvage some of
her gear and machinery and accordingly the company gave notice
that it would entertain sealed proposals to raise the wreck. The
successful bidder, Richard W. Crosset, proposed to employ four
large canal barges and was to receive 70% of what he could realize
from the operations.

---

*H. W. BURTON, *History of Norfolk,* 1877, p. 32-33.

The contract was awarded within a week of the disaster and after working along through the rest of the Spring and Summer with but scant success, the diver was forced to give up and wrote the following pathetic letter to the owners:

M. N. Falls, Esq.

Dear Sir:—Above you will find Bill of Lading for all the articles I have been able to get out of the *North Carolina*. I wish you to pay the freight, and charge it to my account.

It is with feelings of the depest regret that I am compelled to let you know that I have given up all hopes of raising the *North Carolina*. I have striven almost against hope for some time, and I find that the longer I stay the worse it is for me—for I am afraid that this unfortunate affair will be the means of leaving my family houseless, as I see no other way now left for me than to sell my house to raise money to pay what I yet owe on this affair. Five thousand dollars will not leave me in as good circumstances as I was on the 4th day of March last. But if I can get a little time, I hope I shall be able to work through yet. This is the first job I have ever undertaken in my life which I did not finish with credit to myself and satisfaction to my employers; but the fault is not mine, for I cannot fight against the frown of God. The oldest settlers here say they have never seen such a Summer for wind as this has been; the wreck lies in such a bleak place, and so far from land, that the least wind which blows makes such a heavy sea that it is impossible for me to work more than one day out at a time. My barges are very badly strained, and the worms are getting into their bottoms so badly that I am compelled to go home with them.

I will be in Baltimore as soon as I can get my business fixed a little at home. I have to raise some money to settle with my men, &c. Till then, I remain,

Yours respectfully,

R. W. CROSSET.

P. S. Excuse this, as I am scarcely able to hold the pen. I have a severe attack of the fever. God knows how it may end.

R. W. C.

Despite his hard luck, another diver, Isaiah Gifford, made a further attempt to disconnect the machinery later on in the Fall, but he, too, had no success, the water being "as thick as tar, and the tide running as much as five knots." Thus the whole project was abandoned.

The Bay Line's services were much crippled with the loss of the *North Carolina* and almost immediately they set about looking for a steamer to replace her. Their selection fell on a comparatively new wooden side-wheeler, the *Adelaide,* which had been operated by the Calais, Maine, Steamboat Company on the ocean-run between Boston and St. John, New Brunswick. It is interesting to note that this

STEAMER ADELAIDE

Running between Boston, Portland, Eastport and St. John's, N. B.

—*Courtesy of Peabody Museum.*

The side-wheel steamboat *Adelaide* (1854-1880). From the lithograph by Endicott & Co., after a painting by Charles Parsons.

steamer had been designed for a truly "deep water" route, for W. W. Vanderbilt, who ordered her from the Greenpoint, Long Island, builders of Lupton and McDermott, intended to send her out to California, via Magellan Straits, under her own power.

It will be remembered that as a result of the Gold Rush, shallow draft steamers were in enormous demand for use on the Sacramento and other coastwise services in California. The first to arrive, a little ex-Long Island Sound steamboat, the *Senator,* which made the perilous voyage out in '49, proved a bonanza boat for her owners and could command from $40 to $80 a ton for freight, with passenger rates proportionate, and not infrequently gathered in as much as $50,000 on a single trip!* However, the *Adelaide* was deprived of enjoying a similarly glamorous career by being purchased on the stocks for the coast of Maine service.

The *Georgeanna*, built at Wilmington in 1859. From original out-board profile drawing by the builders, the Harlan & Hollingsworth Company.

In size, she was an almost identical steamer to the *North Carolina,* and on her arrival at Baltimore, the crew of the ill-fated ship was assigned to her, bringing her in to Norfolk on her first voyage exactly one month after the former steamer's career was terminated.

Further additions to the Old Bay Line fleet were made the following year when the *Georgeanna* was acquired in March, the *Philadelphia* in July, and the *William Selden* in November, 1860. The former vessel had been built the year before by the Harlan and Hollingsworth Company for G. R. H. Leffler. Discounting the little river boat *Mount Vernon,* the 199-foot *Georgeanna* was the first iron hulled steamer to be employed on the regular run and dispensed with the "hog frame" characteristic of the wooden steamers. It is interesting to note that her employment on the Bay antedated the use of iron hulled passenger vessels on Long Island Sound by several years until the *City of Lawrence* of the Norwich Line appeared in 1867.

The *William Selden,* a slightly smaller wooden steamboat, had been used on the Potomac since her launching in 1851, and had been

*See R. C. McKay, *South Street,* 1934, p. 282-4.

lately employed by the Maryland and Virginia Steam Packet Company (a new organization, not connected, of course, with the Old Bay Line's precursor, the Maryland and Virginia Steam Boat Company) running on the Rappahannock River. In 1853 she had been chartered by the Old Bay Line to run while the *Herald* was undergoing repairs. Henry Burton remarks that on January 25 of that year she established the record between Baltimore and Norfolk of 10 hours and 45 minutes, which, he wrote in 1877, "we don't believe has ever been beaten."*

The *Philadelphia* had been built by Reanie, Neafie & Company for the Old Bay Line's affiliated organization, the Seaboard and Roanoke Railroad, who had established a line of boats running between Norfolk and Seaford, Delaware, on the Nanticoke River in connection with the Wilmington and Baltimore Railroad's Delmarva Peninsula branch. The *Philadelphia* was taken off this run shortly after the Old Bay Line acquired her and they, in turn, chartered her to the Potomac Steamboat Company on October 2, 1860. Some time thereafter they took her off the Old Bay Line's hands entirely. These additions and replacements still left the *Louisiana* the "most commodious" vessel of the fleet which, however, now numbered several excellent modern steamers.

Occasional mention has been made of the excursion business in which the Old Bay Line and other steamboat companies participated. In the Summer of 1860, the Bay Line staged a coup which completely outdistanced all competitors. During July of that year, her owners sent across from England the mammoth steamship *Great Eastern*. This 692-foot vessel, born before her time and considered as nothing short of an eighth wonder of the world, was visited by thousands daily as she lay in New York harbor and accordingly her owners decided to send her out on "barn-storming" cruises to various other Atlantic ports.

The first of these trips was to Cape May, New Jersey, and turned out a complete failure, due to mismanagement. However, crowds

*H. W. BURTON, *History of Norfolk*, 1877, p. 14.

thronged aboard despite a stiff admission charge, and so, even though few passengers signed on for the trip, a second voyage was planned which took the giant liner down to Chesapeake Bay. In the meanwhile officials of the Old Bay Line had not been idle and in return for the inducement of 1,000 tons of coal, the *Great Eastern's* owners granted to the Bay Line the exclusive privilege of placing their passengers aboard the liner for the daylight trip from the Virginia Capes to Annapolis Roads.*

On August 5, weighted down with a full load of excursionists, the *Louisiana* under Captain Russell met the *Great Eastern* off Old Point and transferred her passengers aboard by small boat. The liner then steamed on up to Annapolis while the *Louisiana* and practically everything that floated in Chesapeake Bay followed. On arrival the Bay Line passengers reëmbarked on the *Louisiana* and were returned to Baltimore. Thus, although thousands visited the *Great Eastern,* only the Bay Line passengers got a ride on her. This triumph was extensively advertised in the daily papers under the heading, "Ho! for the *Great Eastern,*" and the round trip, all included, cost only $6.00.†

Burton estimated that 10,000 people came to Old Point for the express purpose of seeing the ship.‡ She was unquestionably the talk of the day and many who viewed her still believed that an iron steamship of that size was not real.

During the twenty years it had been running, the Baltimore Steam Packet Company had been successful in establishing itself in a strong position and had played from the first a major rôle in the history of communications on Chesapeake Bay. The end of the period found the company operating a splendid fleet of up-to-date steamboats which included the *Louisiana, Adelaide, Georgeanna, William Selden, Herald* and *Georgia*[I]. Of a total of some fifteen steamboats which they had owned up to this time, only one, the *Georgia,* remained of their original vessels.

---

*W. A. WALLACE, *The* Great Eastern's *Log,* 1860.
†Baltimore. *Sun,* Aug. 6, 1860.
‡H. W. BURTON, *History of Norfolk,* 1877, p. 40.

—*Courtesy Enoch Pratt Free Library.*

"View of Baltimore City from Federal Hill." The steamboat *Georgia*, one of the first four vessels of the Old Bay Line is shown entering harbor at the right of the print. (After the lithograph by E. Sachse, Baltimore, 1859.)

—*Courtesy The Mariners' Museum.*

"Fortress Monroe, Old Point Comfort and Hygeia Hotel, Va.' The Old Bay Line steamer *Adelaide* (1859-1881) appears in the right foreground of the print. Meteorologists will be amused to note that although the topsail schooner is sailing close-hauled on the starboard tack to a northwest wind, the plume of smoke from the *Adelaide's* funnel indicates that she has a southeast wind. (After the lithograph by E. Sachse, Baltimore, 1861)

Meanwhile many changes had been wrought in the towns and settlements around the route of the Bay Line. The population of both Baltimore and Norfolk had materially increased; Old Point Comfort with its famous Hygeia Hotel had grown to be the most fashionable resort of the South; travel was no longer reserved for the wealthy only; and the ever expanding railroad lines brought an increasing number of passengers and tons of freight to the steamboat wharfs.

All was not well, however. Differences of opinion between North and South were daily increasing and ominous storm clouds gathered on the horizon. It was not to be long before the rifts would widen into bridgeless chasms and hot words would give way to hotter flames and powder. Eighteen-sixty-one dawned and events drew on to an inevitable climax. Abraham Lincoln came to the White House in March and a month later word was brought to Norfolk that the Confederates had opened fire on Fort Sumter in Charleston harbor. Officials of the Bay Line, gateway between North and South, anxiously wondered how it would all turn out.

The War of Secession and its Aftermath

CHAPTER VI

HERE is no place here for a comprehensive history of the naval operations in Chesapeake Bay during the War of Secession, but insofar as possible, mention will be made of those events which directly concerned the Old Bay Line. It should be remembered that when war broke out, the Bay Line's terminal ports were decidedly pro-Confederacy. Norfolk was a Southern city and Baltimore was Southern in sentiment even though Maryland remained in the Union. As the Union Navy gained control of the Chesapeake and blockades were established of Southern harbors, the Bay Line's operations were somewhat curtailed and made to conform to Federal direction. Nevertheless the Line managed to maintain daily service between Baltimore and Old Point Comfort for the duration of the war, and although passenger travel dropped off, there was a large amount of freight to move which, according to Burton,* "paid the line very handsomely" even though northbound shipments of cotton, which had made up a large percentage of cargoes previously, ceased entirely.

The situation of the Federal navy yard at Gosport, [Portsmouth] Virginia, literally surrounded by increasingly hostile country, immediately gave concern to the Union government. The Gosport Yard was unquestionably the most important in the United States and with Virginia proposing to secede, Commodore McCauley felt that it would be better to abandon the post rather than attempt to hold it in the face of eventual and certain hostilities.

Virginia formally withdrew from the Union on April 17, 1861.

*H. W. Burton, *History of Norfolk,* 1877, p. 56-7.

The U. S. Navy intended to send down a large company of naval recruits to put on the warships at Gosport in the attempt either to defend or to withdraw them immediately to safer waters. It was intended to ship these men down via the Old Bay Line, but President Falls wrote Captain W. W. Hunter on the 19th, saying that the company "declined to take them."* Inasmuch as war had not yet been declared between Virginia and the Union, this was a reasonable decision, as the shipment of troops to Portsmouth was an overt act which could only be interpreted in one way.

The very next day, however, those in charge of the Gosport Yard decided to evacuate and the warships which could not readily be moved to Northern waters were destroyed. Included in the systematic destruction of the Yard so that the South might get no benefit from its facilities after the Federal exacuation was an attempt to blow up the drydock and the sinking of several fine vessels including the auxiliary steam frigate *Merrimac*. It will be recalled that later on the Confederates raised what was left of the *Merrimac*, rebuilt her as an ironclad in spite of appalling odds and, re-christened C. S. S. *Virginia,* she fought the Union *Monitor* on March 9, 1862, in the epochal battle of Hampton Roads—the first contest between ironclads.

Norfolk rejoiced at the Federal evacuation of the Yard and an immediate survey clearly showed that the destruction had by no means been complete and that a large part of the guns and stores could be reclaimed for the Confederacy. In the meanwhile the Old Bay Line continued its services from Baltimore to Norfolk with the *Louisiana* and *Adelaide,* but on May 7, the latter steamboat under the command of Captain Cannon was detained at Fort Monroe and required to disembark all passengers and mails. With most of Chesapeake Bay under their control, the Federal naval authorities advised the company that the boats' regular voyages would thereafter terminate at Old Point, but if they wished they might put on a small steamer to run between Old Point and Norfolk. The *William Selden*

Official Records of Union and Confederate Navies, Vol. 4, p. 287.

was sent down for this purpose, but as Norfolk was now declared by the Union to be in a state of blockade, the Confederates retaliated by seizing the *William Selden* when she came into port,* and she remained tied up at Portsmouth for as long as the South was able to hold the harbor of Norfolk.

Shortly thereafter, the Union Navy chartered the *Adelaide* to be used as a transport attached to the Joint Atlantic Blockading Squadron. The most important engagement in which she participated consisted in the bombardment of Forts Hatteras and Clark on August 28 and 29, 1861. Captained by Commander Henry S. Stellwagen, the *Adelaide* together with another former Chesapeake Bay passenger steamboat, the *George Peabody*, carried large numbers of Federal troops down to the Carolina coast and were successful in routing the Confederate batteries supported by the U. S. Navy's gunfire.

The *Louisiana* and *Georgeanna* maintained the regular service down to Old Point through the remainder of the year, but being in need of an additional vessel, the company decided to purchase on February 15 the steamboat *Thomas A. Morgan* from the Delaware River Steam Boat Company. This iron sidewheeler had been built in 1854 by Harlan and Hollingsworth of Wilmington, Delaware, and measured 192 feet in length. On her arrival from the Delaware though, the *Thomas A. Morgan* was immediately brought south and used by the War Department as official mail boat between Fort Monroe and Yorktown. Commanded by Captain Thomas Edgar, she was at Old Point on March 9, and witnessed the famous *Monitor-Virginia* (ex-*Merrimac*) battle.

As the Federal blockade tightened they apparently had no further need for the *Adelaide* and she was evidently returned to the Company. In any event the next year she was on the regular run with the *Georgeanna,* for the U. S. Navy was carrying out experiments on the machinery and boilers of both these boats while they maintained their usual services in 1862 and 1863. The *Georgia*[I]

---

*Official Records of Union and Confederate Navies, Vol. 4, p. 386.

—Courtesy of Bethlehem Steel Co.

Iron side-wheeler *Thomas A. Morgan,* built 1854. From the original outboard profile drawing of the builders, the Harlan & Hollingsworth Company.

and *Thomas A. Morgan* were the only Old Bay Line ships appearing on a list of vessels employed by the War Department in Virginia as of March 11, 1863.*

To all intents and purposes the *Monitor-Virginia* fight was to a draw with neither ship able to destroy the other. As long as they had the C. S. S. *Virginia,* the South was morally in the ascendency, but the turn of events elsewhere made it doubtful that the Confederates could retain Norfolk. The ironclad *Virginia* drew too much water to be taken up the James to Richmond and with so many powerful vessels out to destroy her, and the mouth of Hampton Roads blockaded by U. S. warships and the heavy guns of Fort Monroe, it was obvious that her days were numbered.

When the concentration on Norfolk began, the Union forces entering from the east found no opposition. But before retiring up the west bank of the James, the Confederates, like the Federals the year before, systematically set about destroying the Gosport Yard. As the troops entered Norfolk on May 10, they saw most of Portsmouth in flames and the *Virginia* herself was expressly blown up on

*Official Records of Union and Confederate Navies, Vol. 8, p. 597.

the following day. Along with all other vessels that they were unable to take with them up the James, the Old Bay Line steamer *William Selden,* which had been tied-up for a year, was expressly burned by the evacuating Confederate forces.

With Norfolk captured, the blockade of the Elizabeth River came to an end, but the Bay Line steamers were not permitted to run over the whole of their customary route until the end of the war. Later on in the Fall, though, the company obtained permission from the U. S. Navy to send a tug to Portsmouth in the attempt to recover the machinery of the *William Selden.** No record has come to hand of the success of this venture.

Meanwhile the theatres of the war were being drawn elsewhere and as far as can be ascertained the Bay Line was no longer directly associated with the South's now desperate struggle. Events of minor significance consisted in the attachment of the *Thomas A. Morgan* to the Ware River Expedition on April 10, 1863, and the collision on April 12, 1864, between the *Georgeanna* and the U. S. S. *Iroquois,* caused according to official navy reports because "the pilot put the helm astarboard against regulations."† It is interesting to note that the Old Bay Line claims against the U. S. Government for their use of the *Georgia*[I] and the *Thomas A. Morgan* were not settled until 1896.

On April 9, 1865, the end came at last. General Lee surrendered at Appomattox and peace came to the North and Reconstruction to the war-torn South. The termination of the war found the Old Bay Line, like all other organizations serving the South, in a demoralized state. Passenger traffic had dropped off, resorts were closed, and excursions profitless. The steamers themselves were out of condition, but worst of all was the complete destruction of Southern railways on which the line depended for its freights. With remarkable energy the South attacked the almost hopeless problem of rebuilding its lines and settling down to normal again.

---

*Official Records of Union and Confederate Navies, Vol. 8, pp. 35, 38, 39.
†Ibid., Vol. 9, p. 611.

After peace had been declared, the Bay Line boats once more ran to Norfolk and the mail contract was extended again to cover the whole route. With characteristic energy, the Baltimore Steam Packet Company set about building itself up once more. Anticipating their certain need for new equipment, the company had contracted with the shipbuilding firm of Reaney, Son and Company, Chester, Pennsylvania, for a new iron paddle steamer, 236 feet 9 inches long, to be delivered in five months time. This vessel was christened *Thomas Kelso* after one of the Line's original directors, a prominent citizen of Baltimore then in his eighties.

—Courtesy of The Mariners' Museum.

The wooden paddle steamboat *Eolus*, of Norfolk. Owned by the Old Bay Line from 1864 to 1869.

The Line also acquired in 1865 a little wooden paddler, the *Eolus,* built the year before by Thomas Marvel at Newburg, N. Y. This 144-foot steamboat, commanded by Capt. P. McCarrick, was placed on a newly established feeder day-line from Norfolk to Yorktown, Gloucester, and Mathews County, Virginia, via Old

Point Comfort, three times weekly. On the alternate days she ran across to Cherrystone on the Eastern Shore of Virginia near Cape Charles.

During the war all commercial traffic on the James River ceased, but in the fall of 1865 the Powhatan Steamboat Company was revived by Jacob Brandt, Jr., and operated three steamboats from Baltimore to Richmond. These included the *State of Virginia*[I], *State of Maryland*[I], and *Petersburg,* all of which were later taken over by the Baltimore Steam Packet Company. A newly established Peoples Line covered the same route with the *Agnes* and *Ellie Knight* and the latter vessel was also added later to the Old Bay Line. Steamship services both day and night were also revived between Norfolk and Richmond.

It will be remembered that following the war, when Southern commerce and industry was prostrate, a large number of Northern concerns found the South a ripe field for their endeavor and in the post-bellum period a number of Northern enterprises gained footholds throughout the South. It was only natural, therefore, when the Bay Line was at a low ebb, that a competitor should appear on the scene. The Leary Brothers of New York brought down three steamers which they placed on the Baltimore-Norfolk run with connecting boats for Richmond. As was to be expected a rate war immediately began and the traveling public prospered with fares reduced to $3.00 one way and $5.00 round trip.

As stated in the introduction of this book, the Baltimore Steam Packet Company in the maturity of its years has earned the name of "Old Bay Line." The first time that this name appeared in print occurred on July 24, 1865, when the company's advertisement in the Baltimore *Sun* announced that "The *Old* Established Bay Line" was operating daily the steamers *Louisiana, Georgeanna, Adelaide,* and *Thomas Kelso* from Baltimore to Norfolk with connection at Fort Monroe by the *Thomas Collyer* and *Milton Martin* for James River Landings and Richmond.

The Leary Line's vessels included the *George Leary,* Captain

Blackeman; the *James T. Brady,* Captain Landis; and the *Dictator,* Captain Mulligan. In addition to lowering their fares in the attempt to gather in the patronage which formerly had gone uncontested to the Old Bay Line, the Leary Line offered all sorts of inducements including "bands of musick" to woo travelers and shippers.

—*Courtesy of Mr. E. M. Eldredge.*

Opposition line steamboat *George Leary,* brought in the Old Bay Line fleet in 1867. From the lithograph by Endicott & Co.

Naturally unofficial but highly contested races took place between the rival steamboats and as a result several accidents occurred which probably contributed to the withdrawal of the Leary Line. The *George Leary* rammed and sank a schooner whose entire crew was lost; four days later the *Dictator* ran into a tug in Norfolk harbor and was badly damaged; and a final straw was added when the *George Leary* collided with the *Louisiana* causing the deaths of one passenger and three of the crew.

The Old Bay Line likewise experienced its share of bad luck when the *Thomas Kelso,* Captain Cralle, exploded her steam drum off Wolf Trap Light on the early morning of December 8, 1866, badly scalding her firemen and engineers and injuring several passengers.

However, in January, 1867, the Old Bay Line was successful in buying off its competitor, the steamer *George Leary* being added to its fleet for a consideration of over a quarter of a million dollars, the highest price paid for any one of their steamers up to that time. The other Leary Line steamboats were returned to New York and things returned to normalcy again.

In 1867 John Moncure Robinson succeeded Mr. Falls as fourth president of the Baltimore Steam Packet Company. Mr. Robinson was the son of Moncure Robinson, first chief engineer of the R. F. & P. Railroad, and like most of the Bay Line's officials at this time was a former officer in the Confederate Army. It should be noted here that of the eleven presidents which the Line has had since it began, Mr. Robinson's 26-year tenancy of office has been the longest.

Under his regime the Line was to witness many important changes bringing its ships and services to the state of perfection and efficiency which are associated with modern times. The ships of the Line gradually changed from wooden side-wheelers to iron hulled craft. The screw propeller replaced the cumbersome paddle wheel and, at the last, iron hulls gave way to ships of steel. Steam steering gear replaced the cranky, manually-operated wheels; gas light was abandoned for electricity; pot-bellied stoves gave way to steam-heated radiators. Likewise the high silk hats and frock coats of captains and pursers were discarded for uniforms, first resplendent and gaudy, later more utilitarian and conservative.

As we shall see, these changes did not come over-night, but slowly and inevitably as their efficiency was demonstrated, the Old Bay Line adopted those improvements which kept its fleet at all times at the forefront of American steamboat lines.

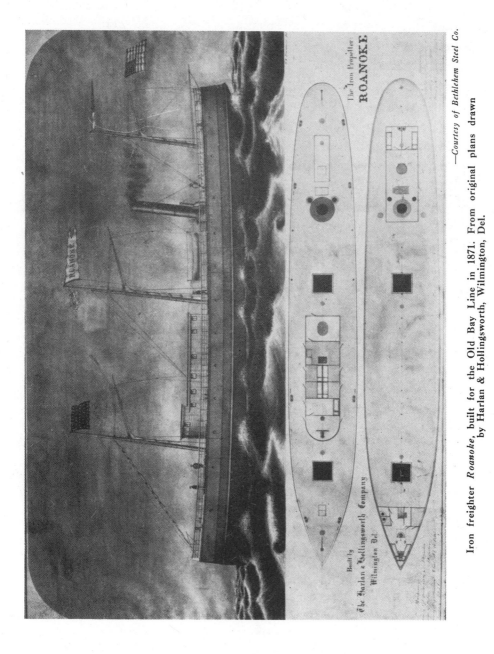

—*Courtesy of Bethlehem Steel Co.*

Iron freighter *Roanoke*, built for the Old Bay Line in 1871. From original plans drawn
by Harlan & Hollingsworth, Wilmington, Del.

The Mosquito Fleet

CHAPTER VII

T the end of the War, the Federal Government had left on its hands a considerable number of small steamboats which had been used as gunboats and transports. With the exception of blockade running and the spectacular cruises of the Confederate commerce raiders *Sumter* and *Alabama,* naval actions of the War became confined to sounds and rivers as the big Union warships succeeded in establishing their effective blockades which bottled up the South. In order to prosecute the conflict the Union forces had acquired a flotilla of boats which were sufficiently small to be effective in narrow waterways, and having no further use for them when peace was declared they were sold to private steamship operators at comparatively low prices.

The three steamboats with which the Powhatan Line resumed service on the James River were all war veterans of this character. Most of the ex-gunboats and transports were converted to freighters and since the Old Bay Line steamers were primarily passenger boats sailing on scheduled service, it was obvious that fleets of small roving freighters would succeed in cornering most of the cargo transportation business since they could readily go where freight offered without delay.

For at least a decade after the end of the War, freight business on the Chesapeake amounted to more than passenger business anyway and it was undoubtedly this factor which determined at this time the acquisition by the Bay Line of their first boats designed to handle cargo only.

Their first freighter and also their first steamboat to be propelled by a screw instead of paddle-wheels was the 305-ton *New Jersey,* built in Baltimore in 1862, which they obtained in 1867 by trading in the *Thomas A. Morgan.* Two years later they acquired a similar wooden hulled propeller steamer, the *Transit,* which had likewise been built during the war for the Montauk, Long Island, Steam Navigation Company. A few months before, the company had sold the *Georgeanna* and *Eolus* together with their almost new steamer *Thomas Kelso,* leaving the passenger business to be handled by the *George Leary, Louisiana,* and *Adelaide.*

The career of the *New Jersey* was short, for on February 26, 1870, she took fire off Sharps Island and was totally destroyed. The company had found that their small freighters were extremely profitable, however, and it was decided to replace the *New Jersey* with a similar screw freighter built of iron. An agreement was effected in June of the same year with the shipbuilding firm of Harlan and Hollingsworth of Wilmington, Delaware, for the construction of a vessel of this type to measure 167.7 feet in length. Harlan and Hollingsworth specialized in iron shipbuilding and although they had built both the *Georgeanna* and the *Thomas A. Morgan,* the new freighter, the *Roanoke,* when it came out in 1871, was the first of many iron steamers expressly built for the Old Bay Line by the Wilmington concern.

Like the freighters which followed it, the black painted *Roanoke* could hardly be classed as a beautiful ship, but although they were obviously ugly ducklings the little freighters were well built and economical to operate. As in modern tankers the machinery and boilers were placed well aft, and since the crew's quarters, galley, and so forth were confined in a narrow deckhouse, practically the entire main deck could be devoted to cargo, in addition to the lower hold. Although ocean steamers continued to carry auxiliary sails almost until the twentieth century, sound and river passenger boats gave up canvas well before the War of Secession. However the Bay Line's new freighters carried three masts and fore-and-aft sails which could help them along in favorable winds.

In 1873-1874 two more new iron freighters were built for the Line. These were the sister ships *Westover* and *Shirley*. A slightly larger freighter, named *Seaboard,* was also built in 1874 and the same year they acquired a little 102-foot side-wheeler, the *Vesta,* which was probably used both as a tug and a transfer steamer in Norfolk harbor, as later on a half interest in her was secured by the Wilmington, Weldon and Seaboard Railroad.

Although these cargo boats could be dispatched entirely as freight offered, the Old Bay Line operated them on pretty definitely established routes, thus the *Transit, Roanoke,* and *Seaboard* were operated between Norfolk to Baltimore with freight from Philadelphia connecting with the Philadelphia, Baltimore, and Washington Railroad at Canton, Maryland, which route became known as the Canton Inside Line. The *Shirley* and *Westover,* named after famous estates overlooking the James River, ran between Baltimore, Petersburg, and Richmond via Norfolk. It will be remembered that the Powhatan Line was operating up the James but as the Old Bay Line was successful in purchasing control of the stock of the Powhatan Line they took over this route and later the three steamers with which the Powhatan Line had inaugurated service in 1865.

Back in 1854 a railroad had been projected to connect Richmond with West Point, then little more than a hamlet at the head of the York River. Just as this was completed the War came along and during its course the line was completely wiped out. At the close of hostilities work went forward to rebuild the railroad and in 1870 the Powhatan Line alternated tri-weekly service on both the James and the York Rivers. Due to the expense connected with its rebuilding, the railroad found itself in bad financial straits and so hopelessly in debt that it was sold under a decree of the Chancery Court to R. S. Burress and Thomas Clyde of Philadelphia. The latter was a very prosperous ship-owner and under his direction a new steamship line was set up between Baltimore and West Point which absorbed the Powhatan Line's York River business.

It would virtually be impossible to trace all the moves and counter moves which took place during the early 1870's by which the control of the various steamboat lines of the York and James Rivers became established. It is quite obvious that the Baltimore Steam Packet's interest in the Powhatan Line was secured merely to protect itself from the competition which threatened if the York River Line became sufficiently well entrenched to take away their Richmond freight business. This move proved but a temporary stopgap, however, for although in so doing the Bay Line acquired the Powhatan Line steamers, when the Richmond and York River Railroad changed hands and the Clyde interests took charge, they established a permanent line with new ships which the Old Bay Line could not disturb.

This new line was incorporated by the Maryland Legislature in 1874 as the Baltimore, Chesapeake, and Richmond Steamboat Company and became the parent of the present Chesapeake Steamship Company. The boats which were brought to the York River were the *Louise, Sue, Havana,* and *Empire.*

Before it was disbanded, the interests of the Powhatan Line personnel were sharply divided between the Old Bay Line and the York River Line. Those favoring the latter naturally came into the Baltimore, Chesapeake and Richmond Steamboat Company but before doing so this faction in the Powhatan Line instigated a lawsuit against the Bay Line charging that,

> Influential shareholders in the Baltimore Steam Packet Company bought a controlling amount of stock in the Powhatan Company and so managed that the Powhatan Company became more and more embarrassed and sold to the Baltimore Steam Packet Company the steamers *State of Virginia, State of Maryland, Ellie Knight,* and *Fannie Lehr.* The bill of complaint is filed to recover damages for the loss in consequence of the alleged breaking up of the business of the Powhatan Company and the subsequent loss of its stock.*

The case was tried at the October term of the Circuit Court in 1875, and adjustments made that were satisfactory. It was of course

---

*Baltimore *Sun,* Sept. 11, 1875, quoted by E. E. LANTZ, *Steamboat on Chesapeake Bay,* Baltimore *Sun,* April 12, 1908.

only natural for the Old Bay Line to make every effort to hang on to the freight business which the new line via the York River threatened. The effort proved both abortive and costly, for in 1875 the Bay Line found itself owner of thirteen vessels which amounted to many more than it could possibly use. These boats were the *Adelaide* and *George Leary* which maintained the regular passenger service, the *Roanoke, Vesta, Shirley, Westover, Seaboard,* and *Transit* which were mostly all new freighters; and the *State of Virginia*[I], *State of Maryland*[I], *Ellie Knight, Cockade City* (ex-*Fannie Lehr*), and *Petersburg* which were all former Powhatan Line ships.

It will be noted that the name of the *Louisiana* does not appear on the roster, for she had been rammed and sunk by the Baltimore-Charleston steamer *Falcon* the year before. This was extremely bad luck for the company for although it owned a veritable navy, only two of the thirteen boats were equipped to handle the regular passenger service. Although launched back in 1854, in 1871 the *Louisiana* had been completely rebuilt and modernized by the shipbuilding firm of William Skinner and Company at a cost of $50,000, which made her still one of the finest steamboats on Chesapeake Bay.

The disaster came about on the night of November 14, 1874, and although the vessel sank in less than forty-five minutes all passengers together with their baggage and the mails were safely transferred to the *Falcon*. Captain Wyndham R. Mayo, who had only joined the line shortly before, was highly praised by the passengers who prepared a testimonial in his behalf.

With the York River Line established and backed by strong financial interests, the competition between it and the Old Bay Line attained startling proportions. One of the first moves of the new company was the invasion of the Norfolk passenger field which, excepting for the brief period of existence of the Leary Line, the Old Bay Line had held uncontested from its beginning. They put two of their boats on a "Peoples Line" which paralleled the Bay Line route. The fare was set at $3.00 one way and as before when direct competition threatened, the Old Bay Line was forced to reduce its tariffs accordingly.

Finally a compromise was reached and by an agreement signed by both Thomas Clyde and John M. Robinson on January 11, 1877, the Peoples Line was discontinued. The Old Bay Line for their part contracted to sell the *Shirley* to the York River Line for three quarters of her initial cost and also agreed to give up any business they might have on the York River together with their interests in a freight line between Baltimore and Philadelphia. The year before they had managed the Seaboard Railroad's steamer *Astoria* on this route for the express purpose of opposing the Clyde interests in the Ericsson Line. Finally, the Old Bay Line agreed to abandon direct service from Baltimore to Richmond and to give up any competition with the outside Clyde Line.

For their part, the Baltimore, Chesapeake and Richmond Steamboat Company agreed not only to keep out of Norfolk but also the James River below the Appomattox and to abandon to the Old Bay Line their feeder interests on the Roanoke, Chowan, and Black Water Rivers in Carolina. The agreement was to be in effect for five years and carried a $75,000 penalty in case of infringement by either party.

The above will give some idea of the far-flung interests with which the various lines surrounded themselves during this critical period of establishing the permanent trade agreements and feeder routes which characterize modern transportation systems.

When those matters quieted down, the Old Bay Line set about reorganizing its fleet of cargo vessels for efficient service and although one freighter, the *Raleigh*[I] was added to the line in 1877, the old boats were either sold or broken up so that in this year its freight fleet included only five boats as opposed to the eleven it had owned two years previously. Meanwhile the Canton Inside Line continued to be profitable and there was other work for Bay Line freighters on the James.

—*Courtesy of The Mariners' Museum.*

Deck plans and profile of the cargo steamer *Gaston,* built in 1881. From the original builders' drawings, Harlan & Hollingsworth Co.

In 1881, Harlan and Hollingsworth provided the Line with another new iron freighter christened *Gaston.* This screw steamer measured 212 feet in length and was driven by a two-cylinder compound steam engine, the first of this type with which a Bay Line boat had been equipped. In direct contrast to the earlier freighters, the *Gaston* was a beautiful little ship, well modeled and of pleasing proportions. President Robinson jokingly referred to her as his "flagship."

In 1884, the New York, Philadelphia, and Norfolk Railroad (now the Delmarva branch of the Pennsylvania) completed its line down the Eastern Shore peninsula to Cape Charles with freight car barge connection across the mouth of the Chesapeake direct to Norfolk. Since the majority of freights became diverted to the new route, the Canton Inside Line was no longer profitable and was forced to suspend operations the following year.

In the meanwhile three new passenger steamers with increased cargo space had been built for the Old Bay Line and a fourth came out in 1887. Since the work of the tramp freighter had been absorbed by the railroads on one hand and regular steamship lines on the other, the "mosquito fleet" came to an end, the Bay Line retaining only the *Seaboard* and *Gaston* for use as auxiliaries to its regular service.

Through the Turn of the Century

CHAPTER VIII

ARS inevitably stimulate advances in the fields of science and invention. Although ships had been built of iron well before the year 1860, nevertheless the famous duel between the ironclads, U. S. S. *Monitor* and C. S. S. *Virginia* proved of enormous significance to iron shipbuilding and the development of naval architecture for commercial craft as well as warships. These advances came to fruition in the comparatively prosperous and expansive period enjoyed by this country following the War of Secession. The South had a very hard time of it, it is true, and its effort to rebuild itself coupled with over optimistic post war prosperity in the North was largely responsible for the financial panic of 1873, but by far the greatest single advance the country had known followed the reunification of the nation.

With iron replacing wood for a considerable part of all new ship construction, it was possible not only to have larger vessels, but also far stronger and more seaworthy ones. In 1869 steam steering engines first appeared on the transatlantic steamship *City of Brussels,* and a single quartermaster could direct the movements of a large ship whereas previously in heavy weather it had taken as many as four men to struggle with a fighting double steering wheel. In 1878, nine years later, another transatlantic liner, the *City of Berlin,* put to sea with a small generator and six electric lights. Underwriters were skeptical at first, considering this an unpredictable fire hazard. Its safety features were soon demonstrated, however, and it was not so many years afterwards that people would refuse to travel on any boat not equipped with electricity.

Not all the pioneering in shipbuilding was reserved for ocean

"Saloon of a Steamboat."
This drawing might well have been made on the Bay Line steamer *Florida.*
From the *Illustrated London News,* May 8, 1875.

going vessels and the Fall River Line steamboat *Pilgrim,* launched in 1883, was not only the first vessel ever built designed to have electricity as the sole means of illumination, but also furnished an early example of the double bottom and watertight compartment construction.

It was immediately following the war that the Fall River Line, under the direction of notorious "Admiral" Jim Fiske, Jr., entered into its own and true "de luxe" travel was born. At the time when the Old Bay Line was trying valiantly to suppress competition and get back on its feet again following the trials of operation in a combat area, the Fall River established itself at the forefront of all Sound steamboat lines. Its two new spotlessly white steamers *Bristol* and *Providence,* coming out in 1869 and costing a million and a quarter each, made the vessels of other lines seem poor and insignificant by comparison. Two Scotch travelers visiting America in the autumn of the same year came up from Fort Monroe to Baltimore and cryptically remarked that on the Bay Line "the accomodation on board was not of the best."* Later on they proceeded to New York and having "dined at the famed Delmonico's, and paid three prices for the privilege," they "embarked on board the steamboat *Bristol* at 5 P. M., en route for Boston, via Fall River."

Describing this vessel in glowing terms they went on to say that:†

> Seven officers in uniform, gold lace and dress boots, receive the passengers as they arrive to embark, porters in white gloves being in waiting to open the carriage doors. Punctually to the time of starting the paddles went round, the splendid band of music struck up, and we were off with the speed of a railway train. Till the shades of evening drew in we enjoyed immensely the lovely scenery on either hand, and then one by one the hundreds of passengers retired to their respective chambers, to be lulled to sleep by the almost noiseless sweep of the vessel on the water, and the sweet low strains of the distant orchestra.

The reader will remember the racial heritage of these travelers which has happily provided the world with an inexhaustible supply

---

*WM. AND W. F. ROBINSON, *Our American Tour,* 1871, p. 119.
†*Ibid.,* pp. 124-5.

of jokes. True to form, they conclude their description with the remark, "All this luxury only costs three cents per mile."

The particular mention of uniformed officers in the merchant service is interesting to note in view of the fact that the Fall River Line was a pioneer in the innovation of uniforming their crews. At this time captains and pursers of the Old Bay and other lines were still wearing their high silk hats and frock coats. Jim Fiske did not stop with dressing up his seamen. Declaring that if Vanderbilt could be a Commodore, he would be an Admiral, he accordingly had a uniform made for himself which would make a regular admiral appear in *mufti* by comparison! For a time he made it a daily practice to be on hand strutting about before the boats sailed and to the "ohs!" and "ahs!" of impressionable lady passengers he "piloted" the steamers around the tip of Manhattan into the East River where a tug came alongside and took him ashore again.

To compete with the luxurious appointments of the Fall River boats all American lines went in heavily for rococo plaster decoration, ginger bread, and gold leaf and in 1875 another foreign visitor remarked that:*

> Boats navigating the rivers and bays of the United States are constructed on a scale of magnificence quite unknown to European waters. . . The grand saloon is not unlike a hall in a palace.

As an illustration we reproduce a contemporary wood-cut view accompanying the above description in a British periodical. As can be seen the main saloon extended two decks high with a dome ceiling, lit by skylights around the sides by day and fancy gas lights by night. The enclosed well containing the machinery divided this saloon from the only slightly smaller forward saloon and cabins led off from both decks. Below in the after hold was situated the "elaborately provided" dining room which could be converted to a dormatory after meals if traffic demanded. Here "crowds of civil negroes, in spotless white jackets, wait at the tables which are ornamented with artificial flowers."† It is interesting to note that it has only been

---

Illustrated London News, May 8, 1875, pp. 433-4.
†*People's Magazine,* London, Jan. 2, 1871, pp. 34-5.

within comparatively recent times that the dining rooms on Sound steamers have been lifted out of the hold and given outside portholes and fresh air.

We have seen that, as a result of the War of Secession, passenger traffic on the Bay fell off heavily and that the various moves made by the lines of the Chesapeake were towards consolidation of freight business. Even though their boats were kept in condition and periodically overhauled, when passenger travel in the South revived, the Old Bay Line was still operating boats of *ante-bellum* construction. With the unfortunate loss of the *Louisiana* coming in 1874, the absolute necessity of embarking on a thorough building program despite the financial depression was made manifest.

The *Florida*[I], the first of the new passenger steamers, was constructed by the Baltimore shipbuilding firm of William Skinner & Son. In size she was approximately the same as the boat she was to replace and being built of wood and equipped with the customary hog bracing, she very much resembled the *Louisiana* in outward appearance as well. In these times a good engine would often survive the wooden hull for which it had been built. One of the ships acquired by the Old Bay Line from the Powhatan Line was the *State of Virginia*[I] originally built in 1849 for use on Lake Erie as the *Northerner*. The old beam engine was apparently still in good condition when the *State of Virginia* was scrapped in 1875 for her machinery was saved and put into the new boat.

The "magnificent" *Florida,* the last wooden boat of the line, began service in the spring of 1876, arriving at Norfolk on her maiden voyage on May 2, in command of Captain Darius J. Hill, "one of the most popular gentlemen ever known to the traveling public."*

In the sumptuousness of her interior fittings, the *Florida* was probably never equalled on Chesapeake Bay and for a decade she floated nightly several thousand square inches of gold leaf through the waters of the States of Maryland and Virginia. Although fast,

*H. W. Burton, *History of Norfolk,* 1877, p. 168.

Iron side-wheel steamer *Carolina*, 1877-1894. The *Carolina*, 1877, and the *Virginia*, 1879, sister ships, were the last of the Old Bay Line's passenger steamers to have paddle wheels. (After a contemporary oil painting formerly owned by President John R. Sherwood.)

she was a crank boat and hard to steer and vibrated so badly that additional bracing had to be installed, the beams for which cut through several staterooms to the annoyance of those passengers to whom they had been assigned.

The *Florida* came out at the time that the new Peoples Line was competing on the Norfolk run with the steamer *Sue* and the Old Bay Line was fortunate in having at this moment a brand new boat as an attraction for passenger travel. The *Louise* was the name of one of the other boats of the Baltimore, Chesapeake and Richmond Steamboat Company and she was used also for excursions out of Norfolk. An account of one of these printed in 1877 shows that times have not much changed for, we learn that, "the trip was greatly enjoyed, and the party returned—nearly all sober."*

The *Florida* was followed by the iron side-wheeler *Carolina,* a Harlan and Hollingsworth product launched in 1877. This new boat likewise made use of a second-hand engine, hers being salvaged from the wreck of the *Louisiana* three years previously. A sister ship, the *Virginia*[I], came two years later, having been built "upon the guarantee that she would outstrip the *Carolina* in a fair race upon the Bay."†

Both *Carolina* and *Virginia* were a little smaller than the *Florida,* but being built of iron and therefore lacking the hog frame, the passenger accommodations and deck space were not cut up. Both regularly made 18 miles an hour, described contemporaneously as "almost the speed of a railroad train." Although they still resorted to hand steering, an innovation of "necessary 'speaking pipes' from pilot house to engine room" was included. Although not originally built with electric lights they had them installed during the first part of the 1880's and were thus equipped with electricity some half a dozen years before incandescent lights came to the White House.

With these three brand new boats in operation, the line had no further need of the *George Leary* and the *Adelaide.* The former

---

*H. W. BURTON, *History of Norfolk,* 1877, p. 170.
†*Semi-Centennial of the Harlan & Hollingsworth Co.,* 1887, p. 274.

Iron side-wheeler *Virginia,* built in 1879. From a contemporary oil painting formerly owned by Chief Engineer T. J. Brownley, now in the possession of his granddaughter.

was sold in 1879 for use on the Potomac River while the latter was taken over by Harlan & Hollingsworth probably as part payment for the new *Virginia.* The *Adelaide* appears as a Long Branch, New Jersey, steamer the next year when on June 19, 1880, she was rammed and sunk in New York Harbor by the *Grand Republic.* Fortunately there were no casualties, for the summer of 1880 proved a disastrous one in the annals of New York shipping and the ghastly *Narragansett-Stonington* collision and fire had claimed an appalling toll.

With the disagreements between the York River Line arranged amicably and new boats in its fleet, the Old Bay Line settled down to a very prosperous period of its existence and on March 15, 1882, its charter was further extended for a forty-year period. Although the work of the tramp freighter had waned, freight movements over the regular line were increasing and the company had plenty of work for the two cargo boats which it had retained in the wind-up of the "mosquito fleet." A stronger bond was being daily forged between the Bay Line and the Seaboard and Roanoke Railroad which delivered its freights from the South, and as early as 1868 it had been announced that both were operated under identical management. President Robinson served in the same capacity for both organizations, as have all succeeding presidents of the line with but one exception.

In this respect the Bay Line's position was further strengthened when in 1889 an association of Southern railroads was formed which later became the system of the present Seaboard Air Line. The roads which thus banded together were the Seaboard and Roanoke, Raleigh and Gaston, Raleigh and Augusta Air Line, and the Wilmington, Charlotte and Rutherford Railroad.

A memorable vessel was built for the company in the year 1887. This was the iron, screw steamer *Georgia*[II], the first boat to have taken the same name as an earlier member of the Bay Line's fleet which had then totaled some thirty-seven steamers since 1840. The *Georgia* was the largest boat which the company had owned up to this time, measuring 280 feet in length and she was also the first passenger steamer to be propelled by a screw. Other noteworthy items of her construction consisted of steam steering gear, steam-heated cabins, and of course electric light throughout.

All the elegance of the "Elegant Eighties" went into her interior accommodations. Deep pile red carpets; gleaming brass spittoons, hand rails, hardware, and grape vine chandeliers; heavy arm chairs and ottomans covered in crimson mohair plush; cherry bedsteads with carved panels and ornamental tops; polished marble slabs on the dressers; mirrors in their begilded frames. Present dictates of good taste would undoubtedly condemn the over-ornate *Georgia,* but for her era the lavishness of her appointments could not have been surpassed and her luxurious bridal suite was the talk of the town. The career of this proud steamboat only terminated a few years ago when, after serving the Bay Line faithfully for twenty years, and Long Island owners for twenty more, plus an interlude as a floating night club in New Haven, she was brought back to her first home port to be scrapped.

With the new *Georgia* added to the line, the cranky *Florida* was withdrawn and held as a spare boat. The company's advertisement issued in 1887 stated that service with the new iron steamers *Geor-*

—*Courtesy of Mr. E. M. Eldredge.*

Steamer *Georgia*, built in 1887. First screw passenger boat of the Old Bay Line.

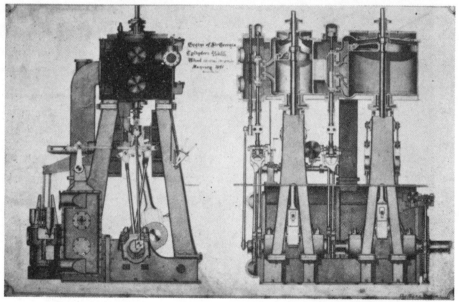

—*Courtesy of The Mariners' Museum.*

Original builders' drawings of the compound steam engine of the *Georgia*, built in 1887 by the Harlan & Hollingsworth Co. These beautifully executed drawings are scarcely comparable to modern blueprints.

gia[II], *Virginia*[I], and *Carolina* was unexcelled, the cuisine unequaled, and that the boats were equipped "with every appointment assuring Luxury, Comfort, and Reliability."*

---

*R. W. Lamb, *Our Twin Cities—Norfolk and Portsmouth*, 1887-8, p. 214.

The improvements brought to the service by the addition of the *Georgia* again gave the Line an unbalanced fleet and accordingly it was decided to build her a similar running mate at an early opportunity. This plan was carried out in 1892 with the construction of the *Alabama*[II] at the yard of the Maryland Steel Company. If the *Georgia* had been considered to epitomize the arts of the shipwright on Chesapeake Bay, the new *Alabama* carried the standard to new heights. She was not only larger and faster but also had a steel hull, a decided improvement over iron construction. Propelled by a single screw, the *Alabama* was equipped with a four-cylinder triple-expansion engine of the same type and size as in modern Bay Liners. Her licensed capacity was 400 passengers and she had 110 staterooms "tastefully decorated in white and gold."

The *Alabama,* christened by Miss Champe Robinson, daughter of the Line's president, slid down the ways into the Patapsco on October 1, 1892. She made 19½ miles an hour on her trials early the next year and joined the line on April 17. The late Samuel Ward Stanton, then editor of *Seaboard Magazine* (now *The Nautical Gazette*) and an authority on American steamers of all types, called her not only a "peerless addition to the Chesapeake Bay fleet" but also the "finest passenger boat ever turned out for service" on that body of water.*

The addition of the *Alabama* gave the company two fine new screw steamers leaving the terminal ports of Baltimore and Norfolk nightly every day in the week except Sunday. The side-wheel *Virginia* was retained as the extra boat of the line and the *Carolina* and *Florida* were sold. The former was purchased by the Richelieu and Ontario Navigation Company and operated on the St. Lawrence River in Canada, first under her old name and later as the *Murray Bay* and the *Cape Diamond* until 1932. The *Florida,* cantankerous to the last, was sold to James H. Gregory of New York for $3,500 to be broken up. On the way north, however, she sank at the end of

---

Seaboard Magazine, New York, Oct. 6, 1892, p. 815. Also, S. W. STANTON, *American Steam Vessels,* 1895, p. 454-5.

—*Courtesy of The Mariners' Museum.*

Steamer *Alabama,* built in 1893. From an advertising lithograph issued by the company. It is amusing to note that in order to make the *Alabama* seem larger, the people on deck are drawn about the size of dwarfs—an advertising trick commonly practiced half a century ago.

the towline off Atlantic City on the stormy afternoon of April 28, 1892, and even what little scrap value she had was thus lost.*

The same year that the *Alabama* came out, the company had a small steam tug, the *Elsie,* built in Baltimore for its use in Baltimore harbor in docking the passenger ships, moving barges, and other work. This gave a total of six vessels owned by the line in 1893.

It is no discredit to the present management to point out that the 1890's, for the Bay Line as well as for most other American steamboat lines, undoubtedly represented its heyday. Florida was yet to be heard from and the hotels and resorts around Hampton Roads attracted scores of winter vacationists. Automobile travel had not been born and the proud steamboats of the era captured the cream of fashionable travelers. Naval architects had evolved splendid safe and seaworthy vessels, sufficiently fast to satisfy a nation still not yet drunk with a mania for speed.

*See Baltimore *Sun,* April 29, 1892, p. 4.

It was at this time that the Old Bay Line, long famous for its meals, was offering its celebrated $1.00 à la carte dinner. This feast started in with Mobjack Bay oysters and including such delicacies of the season as diamond-back terrapin, canvas-back duck, quail, Norfolk spot, turkey, beefsteak, and all of the best of seafood and game which could be obtained in the epicurean paradise surrounding the waters of the Chesapeake. One old gentleman who has been traveling on the Old Bay Line since 1868 has written to advise me that his favorite portion was a dish of oyster fritters cut into small pieces and fried in butter. "My, how good they did taste!" he concluded nostalgically. Even though the meals furnished on board Bay Line boats are good today, canvas-back and terrapin have forever vanished from the scene.

Mr. Watson Sherwood, a son of the then General Manager of the Line, has been good enough to furnish the following word-picture of early times as he remembers them:

> In its heyday, about fifty years ago, the Old Bay Line was, if I recall correctly, the only quick connection between the North and the South. The traveler from New York was brought in to Baltimore by the Pennsylvania Railroad to a junction on the eastern outskirts of the city where his car was detached from the train and brought into the Bay Line wharf at Canton.
>
> The purser whom I most clearly recall was Mr. Charles Spotswood of Norfolk, a typical Virginia Cavalier. When he sold a passenger his ticket and selected his stateroom it was like a court ceremony. Captain Bohannon of the *Alabama* was a magnificent figure of a man from Mathews County, Virginia, who always stationed himself in the social hall both to welcome his passengers coming aboard and, the next morning, to bid them goodbye.
>
> The bartender on the *Alabama* was John Page Harris, dead these many years, but whose son, Willie Harris, is still a waiter on the *President Warfield*. I think that John Harris, a colored man, must have come from Ethiopian stock because he had the bearing and dignity of royalty.
>
> In those days life was leisurely and we have lost forever a way of living and a mental attitude which the people of today will never know.

The serenity of the above picture was shattered when in 1896 the Southern Railroad, which had by this time absorbed the management

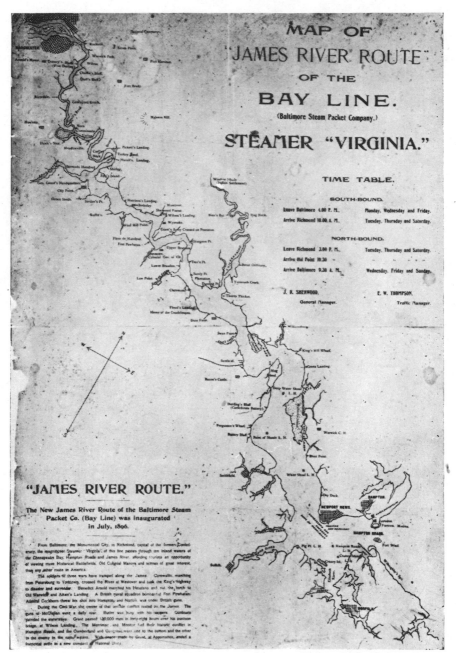

—*Courtesy of The Mariners' Museum.*

Map of the Old Bay Line's James River Route inaugurated in 1896 to oppose
the Chesapeake Line.

of the Baltimore, Chesapeake and Richmond Steamboat Company, transferred its terminal from West Point to Pinner's Point on the Elizabeth River directly opposite Norfolk in the outskirts of Portsmouth.

Claiming that the agreement with the Baltimore Steam Packet Company whereby they abandoned their Peoples Line to Norfolk had expired in 1881, The York River Line prompted by the Southern Railway diverted two of its passenger steamers, the *Charlotte* and the *Atlanta,* to the Baltimore-Norfolk run in direct opposition to the Old Bay Line. The latter naturally protested, claiming that at least a gentleman's agreement was still in force and the opening guns of a major rate war were sounded as competition waxed hotter at every contact.

One of the first of the Old Bay Line's moves was an attempt to re-enter the Richmond trade, figuring that if their rivals had broken their part of the agreement that their own promises to keep off the York River territory were thereby made invalid. The *Georgia*[II] and the *Alabama*[II] were on the regular service and as the side-wheel *Virginia*[I] was being held as alternate boat for excursions and charters and to replace the regulars when they underwent periodic overhauls, she was immediately prepared to undertake direct service from Baltimore up the James to Richmond, thrice weekly. This all-water route would undoubtedly take away some of the York River Line's transhipped freight at West Point.

The first trip of the *Virginia* on the "New James River Route" of the Old Bay Line was scheduled to leave Baltimore on July 17, 1896, with arrival at Richmond after an eighteen-hour run. Company circulars advertised in flowery terms the scenic beauties of the mighty James and the close bond of fellowship that would be cemented between Baltimore and the capital of Virginia. These fooled nobody, however, and Richmond newspapers unabashedly announced that a "lively" rate war was promised.* This became a reality when the Bay Line announced that its fare would only be

*Richmond *Dispatch*, July 16, 1896, p. 3.

$2.00 one way between Baltimore and Richmond and $3.00 round
trip. Meanwhile of course the York River Line was forced to
follow suit, just as the Bay Line was compelled to meet the rate cut
with the rival line on its regular run.

Commanded by Captain William Porter, the *Virginia* laden with
notables left Baltimore on schedule and churned its paddles furiously
so as to arrive within the alotted time. Richmond was pleased to
welcome the new line and the *Virginia* was described in glowing
terms as being a superior boat, very fast, with accommodations for
three hundred passengers and safeguarded at night by a 10,000
candlepower searchlight.

The *Virginia* arrived safely on the morning of July 18, having
been delayed slightly by grounding below Richmond. This omen
presaged worse luck to come. The same afternoon, after the speeches
of welcome had been delivered by the reception committee, she left
her dock for the return trip to Baltimore. Only a few miles down
the James she grounded again and then drove on a rock below Dutch
Gap and stuck fast. It was obvious that she would not come off in a
hurry and one can well imagine the chagrin of the officials as their
first boat load of passengers was returned to Richmond on board
a tug.

The newspapers of July 21 announced that "the rate war goes
merrily on, another fierce cut was made yesterday." The *Virginia*
was still defying all efforts to dislodge her and the same article
observed that she was "wedged in between two rocks that would not
hold her better had they been made for the purpose."*

Having inaugurated the new line with such fanfare, it was im-
perative that a successor be found for the *Virginia* right away. As
all their passenger boats were in service, the Old Bay Line was
forced to look elsewhere for a suitable charter. They first obtained
the old side-wheeler *Enoch Pratt* and she was immediately dispatched to Richmond, but arrived so hopelessly behind schedule that
it was obvious she could not begin to fill the bill. The company next

---

*Richmond *Dispatch*, July 21, 1896.

got hold of the propeller *Tred Avon,* a somewhat larger and faster steamboat used on the Choptank River, but she took twenty-six hours to come down which was eight hours in excess of the schedule the Old Bay Line hoped to maintain. Temporarily giving up the passenger business as a bad job, they put on their own freighter, the *Gaston,* to handle only cargo until such time as the *Virginia* could be restored to service.

In the meanwhile the Merritt Wrecking Company succeeded in getting off the *Virginia* and she was immediately towed down the river to Newport News and put in the one large dry dock operated by the new shipbuilding firm. The damage was considerable, but fortunately not serious. Forty feet of keel plates were torn off leaving six ribs entirely exposed, but the water-tight hull was still intact and unstrained. A repair crew was put on the job right away and the success of their efforts is evidenced by the following article which appeared in a trade journal shortly afterwards.*

> The Newport News Shipbuilding and Dry Dock Company, as is well known, has one of the largest and most complete shipyards in this country. It is specially equipped for rapid repair work and demonstrated this fact recently when the steamer *Virginia,* of the Old Bay Line, was placed in its dock for repairs. The *Virginia's* bow was badly damaged by striking a rock in the James River. As soon as placed in the the dry-dock a force of men was put to work on her, and operations were carried on night and day, electric lights being used after dark. As a result she was completely repaired in a remarkably short time considering the extent of the damages, and again placed in commission as good as new. It is claimed that this is one of the quickest pieces of repair work which has ever been accomplished by any company in this country. In fact, the work was done sooner even than the superintendent of the shipyard estimated, by several days.

On July 31, having been off the line for only two weeks, the *Virginia* resumed her tri-weekly service on the James, tariffs reaching an all-time low with the fare between Richmond and Baltimore, normally costing about $8.00, reduced to a single dollar. Meanwhile on the regular run the *Georgia* and *Alabama* continued to offer stiff competition to the smaller Chesapeake Line boats *Charlotte* and

Manufacturers Record, Aug. 21, 1896.

Atlanta and for the third time since 1840, the names "Old Bay Line" and "New Bay Line" accompanied all advertisements.

At the time it looked as if the Old Bay Line, despite its initial setback, would be permanently committed to the James River "new" line. Although navigation as far up as City Point was comparatively simple, above the confluence of the Appomattox and the James, the channel thence to Rocketts landing below Richmond was so narrow and tortuous that a repetition of the *Virginia's* first misadventure seemed inevitable. Accordingly the company contracted with Harlan & Hollingsworth in 1897 for a new steel steamer, 245 feet in length, and equipped with twin screws which would render her capable of manouvering quickly in the narrow, twisting waterway.

It was obvious that this time rivalry on the Chesapeake was there to stay and equally obvious that with tariffs cut to the bone that neither organization could hope to keep going. Accordingly the companies got together once more and agreements were reached whereby rates were again restored to normalcy. The Chesapeake Steamship Company reorganized from the Baltimore, Chesapeake and Richmond Steamboat Company in 1900 has, however, continued to maintain a service down Chesapeake Bay which exactly parallels that of the Old Bay Line. The last Old Bay Line trip on the James took place on December 31, 1897, and three years later the old sidewheel *Virginia* was sold. After passing through several hands she went to join her sister the *Carolina* in Canadian waters.

The new twin-screw steamer named *Tennessee* was completed after the Old Bay Line had come to an understanding with its rival and so was never given an opportunity to put to the test the manouvering ability for which she had been expressly designed. She was also smaller than the boats assigned to the regular run and when an opportunity came along to dispose of her to advantage in 1906, she was sold to the Long Island Sound Joy Line in whose service she was described as "one of the best little sea boats Point Judith ever tackled."* The *Tennessee* sported an elegant, golden eagle on top

*R. W. McAdam, *Salts of the Sound*, 1939, p. 192.

—*Courtesy of Mr. E. M. Eldredge.*

Twin screw steamer *Tennessee,* owned by the Old Bay Line from 1898 to 1906.

of her pilot house and, as was customary in an age not completely given over to utilitarian considerations, her stem was decorated with gilded, carved arabesques, a survival of the day when sailing ships had their figureheads and trail-boards. Her career was terminated in Boston Harbor on September 9, 1936, when as an excursion steamer renamed *Romance* she was rammed and sunk by the Eastern Steamship Line's *New York.*

It was obvious to Bay Line officials that the activities of the Chesapeake Line would seriously diminish the volume of business which they had previously handled uncontested and that their fleet would have to be proportionately reduced. The first move after peace had been declared was to sell the iron freighter *Seaboard,* then almost twenty-five years old. This venerable craft joined the fleet of the Hartford and New York Transportation Company and regularly carried freight and passengers from New York to Bridgeport, Conn., until 1930. For three years thereafter she lay in an abandoned slip until a new purchaser came along and rebuilt her as a coastwise tanker. Her original iron hull was covered with quarter-inch soft steel plates arc-welded into place. A large percentage of frames and beams were renewed, but essentially she was still the same old boat. A steeple compound steam engine which had replaced her original simple cylinder at some intermediate period of her career was removed and a modern Worthington diesel installed. The *Seaboard* according to latest reports is still owned and operated out of Providence, R. I., and her sixty-six odd years' service makes her one of the oldest steamers afloat today under American registry.

On the night of May 17, 1898, a fire of undetermined cause swept through and completely destroyed the company's establishment at Union Dock at the foot of Concord Street, Baltimore. The buildings were horseshoe-shaped with berthing facilities for several steamers. Sixteen hundred bales of cotton, over fifty hogsheads of tobacco, and other freights awaiting shipment were destroyed as well as a large percentage of the early records of the Line. The schedule followed at that time called for departure from Union Dock at 6:30 P. M., southbound, with a brief call at Canton to pick up through passengers arriving by train. The incoming *Alabama* docked the next morning at Pier No. 10, Light Street, and despite the setback, service went on from there without interruption.

Shortly thereafter, the company acquired permanently the Light Street property with a 274-foot frontage and erected the buildings surmounted by the tower which are familiar to travelers today. Their present quarters were badly damaged in the famous Baltimore Fire of February 7, 1904, and then again by similar cause in 1911, but on each occasion the buildings were rebuilt to conform to their original design, a clock with four faces being added to the celebrated tower after 1911.

Prior to the fire of 1904 which destroyed an enormous section of down-town Baltimore, Light Street was narrow and crowded. When the company's new buildings were completed just prior to the end

—Courtesy The Old Bay Line.

The Old Bay Line's dock at Pier No. 10, Light Street, Baltimore. From a photograph taken shortly after the Baltimore Fire in 1904, when Light Street was widened.

of the century they constructed an overpass and it was stated that:*
"by means of this bridge, passengers are not compelled to cross the bed of Light Street, thereby avoiding the risk of being knocked down by the many teams that surge through the thoroughfare"—a hazard which Baltimoreans will agree is equally applicable today.

The congestion had become truly critical and when the waterfront properties were rebuilt in 1905, the city authorities wisely decided to widen Light Street by condemning real estate on the west side of the thoroughfare. In the process the Old Bay Line's overpass was torn down, but even though its life had been short, it had well justified its existence and probably prevented a considerable number of accidents. It is unfortunate that it has never been rebuilt.

President Robinson's long term in office was terminated by his death in 1893. Richard Curzon Hoffman succeeded to this post and continued in command during the critical period of adjustment with the Southern Railroad and the Chesapeake Line until his resig-

---

*History of Baltimore, 1902, pp. 123-4.

nation in 1899. John Skelton Williams was then elected president, holding office for five years. At the turn of the century, despite the permanent rivalry of the Chesapeake Line, the Old Bay Line was in good condition and was operating the passenger steamers *Alabama*[II], *Georgia*[II], and *Tennessee;* the freighter *Gaston;* and the tug *Elsie.* The new docks, warehouses, and offices were an enormous improvement over the old and the outlook for the new century was bright.

The Dawn of Modern Times

CHAPTER IX

HORTLY after the 1900's began, the Seaboard Air Line Railway acquired the entire capital stock of the Baltimore Steam Packet Company and although the Bay Line preserved its individuality in operation and management, nevertheless it thus became a unit in a large transportation system. A large number of American steamboat lines operating coastwise and on sounds and inland waterways were owned by one railroad line or another. Although this was advantageous in a great many respects, later, upon the passage of the Panama Canal Act, it could be the instrument of bringing a real hardship to such boat lines for, under that law, rail-owned steamboats could not immediately vary their charges to meet outside competition, as could non-rail owned lines.*

Inasmuch as the Old Bay Line was a very necessary northern link of the Seaboard system and since there were no independent boat lines paralleling it, this trouble was not experienced and reciprocally profitable and pleasant relations existed between the Bay Line and the Seaboard.

The same railroad ownership applied to the Chesapeake Line, as later both the Southern and the Atlantic Coast Line held the capital stock in its corporation. This meant that although competition between the Chesapeake and the Old Bay Lines was keen, particularly with respect to local passenger traffic, the competing railroad systems provided each of their lines with through freight.

*In 1916, the Panama Canal Act prohibited parallel rail and boat lines under the same ownership. The Interstate Commerce Commission approved, however, rail-owned steamboat lines where there was no parallelism. This sanctioned the operation of both Old Bay and Chesapeake Lines under railroad ownership.—Baltimore *Sun,* August 28, 1916.

With the transfer of its terminals from West Point to Portsmouth the importance of the Chesapeake Line's York River service diminished in direct proportion to the increase of their Norfolk business. Their *Charlotte* and *Atlanta* had inaugurated the new line and in 1900 they added a new steamer, the *Augusta,* to the Baltimore-Norfolk service. The *Augusta* was larger than their old boats and being a "two-piper" she was a distinctive looking craft and well

—*Courtesy of Mrs. Perry Fuller.*

Launching party of the steamer *Virginia,* 1905. President Sherwood is at the left wearing a panama hat.

appointed inside. It is said that she introduced to Chesapeake Bay the innovation of brass double beds in the better cabins.

Although the Old Bay Line was operating larger boats, a brand new vessel was always a heavy drawing card for passengers and the *Augusta* proved a popular ship. The Old Bay Line's *Tennessee,* especially built for the James River, was their latest vessel but being considerably smaller than the *Georgia* and *Alabama,* she was thus unsuitable for a balanced fleet. In 1905 the company decided to build a new steamer slightly larger than the *Alabama.* This vessel, the *Virginia*[II], was constructed by Harlan & Hollingsworth and given the same name as the iron side-wheeler sold in 1900. On

—Courtesy of Bethlehem Steel Co.

Screw freighter *Raleigh*, built in 1906 by the Maryland Steel Company. From a painting by Antonio Jacobsen.

completion, this 296-foot steamer joined the *Alabama* on the regular run, the *Georgia* became the spare boat, and the *Tennessee* was sold.

Freight was picking up and since the Bay Line then only had one cargo boat, the *Gaston,* they chartered the *City of Philadelphia* to help her out in 1904, and two years later built the *Raleigh*[II], a fine modern steel freighter. Meanwhile the Chesapeake Line decided that they could use a new boat and their new *Columbia* coming out early in 1907 was a worthy rival of the *Virginia* to the title "Queen of the Chesapeake."

The Jamestown Tercentennial Exposition held during 1907 at specially prepared grounds near Sewell's Point, Norfolk, brought an unprecedented increase in passenger traffic to both lines. The old rivalry between them flared up and manifested itself in numerous unofficial races between the *Virginia* and the *Columbia*. The most exciting of these took place on September 11, 1907, and though technically "unofficial" the outcome was anxiously awaited in both camps. Both ships were carrying full passenger lists of Exposition tourists. The *Columbia* got away from Baltimore first and maintained her lead almost until Old Point Comfort, when the *Virginia,* less deeply laden with cargo, was able to take a short-cut across the "Horseshoe" bar and got to Norfolk with a ten-minute lead over her rival. As the *Columbia* had left Baltimore ten minutes before the *Virginia,* this still left open the question as to which boat was the winner, which point could be, and was, heatedly argued on both sides.*

It is interesting to note that in the year of the Exposition, the Old Bay Line carried some 107,217 passengers, a staggering gain of over 48,000 previously transported. Further statistics are not without interest: in 1906 the steamers of the Bay Line traveled a total of 163,999 miles—a distance equal to approximately six and a half times around the world.

—Courtesy The Old Bay Line.

Steel Screw Steamer *Florida.* Built by the Maryland Steel Company in 1907 and today an automobile ferry at San Francisco. (From a contemporary advertising lithograph, by A. Hoen & Co., Baltimore.)

The new *Virginia* was followed in 1907 by a new *Florida*[II], built by the Maryland Steel Company, builders of the *Alabama.* She was completed too late to take part in the Jamestown Exposition traffic, but her speed of twenty-one miles an hour automatically gave her the title of "Queen of the Chesapeake" without the necessity of a race to prove it.†

*Baltimore *Sun,* Sept. 11, 1907. Baltimore *News,* Sept. 18, 1907.
†See: "The fast steamer *Florida";* in *International Marine Engineering,* New York, April, 1908, pp. 145-8.

Both the new *Florida* and *Virginia* had reciprocating steam plants similar to the *Alabama,* and although turbines were considered in the case of the *Florida,* it was finally decided to install the old type engine so that the "black gangs" might readily be transferred from one ship to another without any lost motion due to lack of familiarity with the newer type. The new boats were beautifully finished in Elizabethan style, the main saloons and galleries being done in cream and gold with mahogany trimmings, while the dining rooms and social halls had quartered oak and interlocking rubber tiling floors.

The *Florida* was slightly larger than the *Virginia,* having 136 staterooms as opposed to 110. In 1909 both *Alabama* and *Virginia* had additional after galleries added and the staterooms increased to the same number as the *Florida.* In both cases this entailed extensive alterations and the hurricane decks were carried right out to the extreme stern. With these improvements effected, the Old Bay Line for the first time in its career had three up-to-date screw steamers which were to all intents and purposes identical in size, speed, and passenger and freight accommodation.

One additional feature of the newest of the boats, the *Florida,* was the illumination of the main saloons by handsome domes piercing the gallery deck and glazed with cathedral glass. The company had every reason to be proud of its modern fleet and rightfully advertised them as the "finest and fastest steamers south of New York," and in 1912 the president of the company wrote to Mr. H. S. Meldrum, then chairman of the board, that "our steamer *Florida* is looking just beautiful!"

The same year that these improvements had been made in its fleet the Old Bay Line sold the *Georgia*[II], since the two regular steamers with their one alternate were all that were needed to handle the passenger service. The old *Georgia* had been very useful to the company as a day excursion steamer during the summer of the Jamestown Exposition and many old friends regretted it when she went to join the *Tennessee* on Long Island Sound.

The year 1909 was another busy one for the Old Bay Line, the chief drawing card being the arrival at Hampton Roads of the United States Fleet after its noteworthy round-the-world cruise. During the Summer of this year, the Old Bay Line fitted out all three of its passenger steamers with "the Marconi Wireless," installed by the United Wireless Telegraph Company, which made its boats the first to be so equipped on Chesapeake Bay. A contemporary account stated that wireless communication between ship and shore would be highly favored by traveling business men, but that it would hardly prove popular with young couples attempting to elope secretly on the Old Bay Line.*

Although both Old Bay and Chesapeake Lines had come to an agreement with respect to tariffs, nevertheless the competition held rates to a minimum and the prices charged in 1909 were $3.00, one way from Baltimore to Norfolk, and $5.00, round trip. To Richmond, via Bay steamboats and boats of the Virginia Navigation Company operating on the James, tickets cost $3.50, and there was also a "second class" fare Baltimore to Norfolk of $2.00.

In 1907, John R. Sherwood, who had already served almost forty years with the Line, was elected President and General Manager, breaking the precedent which formerly had given to the president of the Seaboard the presidency of the Bay Line. "Captain" Sherwood was a very popular choice for this post and in his former capacity of vice-president, in charge of operations, he had been largely responsible for the new steamers which added so much to the efficiency of the line's operations.

During the summer of 1910, due to the pressure of an extraordinary volume of perishable food movements, it was decided to put the boats on Sunday trips in addition to the daily ones through the week. The trucking business in season amounted to the greater part of freight shipped via Old Bay Line and the scruples against "desecrating" the Sabbath, in vogue in 1840, found no place in these, the dawn of modern times. Both lines then regularly ran Sunday boats

*Baltimore *Sun,* June 19, June 25, 1909.

although by the Old Bay Line the service was suspended through the winter until as late as 1931.

Having had ample opportunity of observing the efficiency in operating practically identical boats, the Chesapeake Line under the presidency of Mr. Key Compton, former traffic manager of the Old Bay Line, decided in 1911 to build a pair of new steamers for the Norfolk run. When the new steamers, *City of Baltimore* and *City of Norfolk,* costing a total of well over a million and a half dollars, came out the Old Bay Line was faced with one of the most serious situations in its career. The new Chesapeake Liners were considerably larger and had added an entirely new deck, which placed their pilot houses three decks above the main deck, on Sound class steamers the one which comes first above the waterline. At best, passenger traffic is a fickle miss to woo and the new boats of the rival line attracted many new passengers.

Prior to this embarrassment had come the fire to their premises in Baltimore on February 2, 1911, fortunately covered by adequate insurance. For a time the Bay Line went back to using Union Dock vacated in 1898 until their new buildings could be repaired.

Although for the moment outclassed by the new Chesapeake Line steamers, the Old Bay Line had during 1911 two opportunities to demonstrate that as far as seamanship was concerned it would retain its customary place second to none. The first of these occurred on the night of May 11, when the watch on board the *Florida* observed a fire in the vicinity of Poplar Island. Several other steamers had seen the blaze, but had gone on their way judging it to be a brush fire ashore. Captain W. C. Almy, however, decided to go out of his way to investigate and after steering four miles off his course, he came upon four men clinging to a sea-swept raft while their schooner, the *Nellie Ruark,* blazed to her waterline. A boat was lowered and in short order the miserable survivors "more dead than alive" were brought aboard the *Florida.*

A similar rescue of five men from the waterlogged launch *Smiles* took place on November 13. The men were waving a red lantern as

signal of distress but were not observed until the *Florida* came along.
A forty-five mile gale was blowing and it proved a ticklish procedure
to back the *Florida* around to make a lee so that a line could be sent
to the launch to tow her alongside. In the process the *Florida* got
into shallow water and grounded, but came off without trouble after
the rescue had been effected.

Naturally, official recognition was made of these events, President Sherwood concluding his annual report to the stockholders on
March 31, 1912, with the statement that,

> In both of these instances other vessels had passed them, which I think
> makes it more commendable to Captain Almy and his crew in keeping
> a sharp lookout.

Further recognition took place on August 5, 1912, when William
B. Hurst, a director of the company, made a presentation of medals
to Captain Almy; First Officer R. S. Foster (now senior commander
in the Bay Line); Second Officer George U. McGrath; Lookout
Floyd Miles; Watchman E. Johnson; and Ernest Seldon and Albert
White, colored waiter and deckhand respectively.*

To balance the score, the *Virginia*[II] likewise performed her
good deed and in the minutes of the company of December 18 there
appears a resolution of thanks,

> . . . tendered to Captain W. G. Lane, his officers and others instru-
> mental in prompt relief afforded the passengers of the steamer *Atlantic*
> of the Eastern Shore Development and Steamship Company on the
> morning of December 8, 1912, when sixteen passengers, three of whom
> were women, were taken from the disabled steamer which was lying
> near Bloody Point, and transferred to the steamer *Virginia* and brought
> to Baltimore.

Due to a succession of extremely severe winters, Old Bay Line
mariners were given other opportunities of demonstrating their seamanship. Nineteen hundred and five had been a bad year, ice in
the Bay causing the loss of ten round trips in the month of February
alone. Nineteen hundred and nine was similar and the jagged floes
were piled up like icebergs, and in some places the Bay appeared an

---

*See *Old Bay Line Magazine*, Sept. 1912, pp. 1-3.

unbroken ice field. With their steel hulls acting like sounding boards, the noise and vibrations as the steamers ground their way laboriously along were not condusive to the good night's sleep which advertising copy promised.

Probably due to excessive straining, on one occasion the steering gear of the *Florida* became out of order and for a few moments she had a gay time running amôk in the Elizabeth River before she could be gotten under control. These derelictions of duty were so rare, however, that they may be mentioned without embarrassment. Three years later another slight mishap occurred when the *Florida* grounded while looking for a place to anchor in a snowstorm. At the time the ice in the Bay was in some places five and six feet thick.

Even though the Chesapeake Line was operating fine big new boats, the Old Bay Line kept its three steamers in the best of condition and they were periodically overhauled and modernized. Jarman refrigeration plants were installed on the *Virginia* and *Florida* in 1912 and the number of lifeboats carried per steamer was increased from six to twelve. Passenger travel was light in 1912, due in all probability to the disaster to the *Titanic* on April 14, an event which affected waterlines all over the world. As a result of this, stiffer government inspection laws were passed, but it is worthy of mention that in increasing its safety appliances the Old Bay Line acted long before laws were passed which made this obligatory.

Between the years 1910 and 1918, the company published a monthly periodical entitled *The Old Bay Line Magazine,* edited by Alfred I. Hart of Baltimore. Topical articles of all kinds were carried and there was a department entitled "Briny Breezes" in which stock jokes of the day were printed. Some of these jocose items were pretty sad, it is true, but the little magazine was a pleasant one and furnished passengers free entertainment and was a good advertisement for the line even if such obvious "plugs" as "the menu has defied the criticism of the most fastidious epicureans" were printed.*

Old Bay Line Magazine, January 1913.

The volume of business enjoyed by American transportation lines doubled as a result of war in Europe and when later the United States joined the Allies, the Old Bay Line ships ran capacity loads of both passengers and freight. Of the three wars in which this country had been engaged since the Old Bay Line began, two of them, the Mexican in 1846 and the Spanish in 1898, had little effect on the operations of the Bay Line. However, like the War of Secession, the Great War, although well removed from Chesapeake Bay, made a decided mark on the management of the line. The port of Hampton Roads, always an important entrepôt of trade, increased its activities enormously as whole communities mushroomed into being on its shores. Despite an exceptionally bad winter in 1917, in which the Bay was frozen solid for six weeks, the Old Bay Line transported 107,664 people during the year, a large number of whom were soldiers and sailors.

As a war measure, on January 1, 1918, the United States Government took over the management of all American railroad and steamboat lines and for convenience in operation, the Federal transportation authorities decided to combine both the New and the Old Bay Lines. Under the consolidation, Mr. Key Compton, president of the Chesapeake Line, was appointed Federal Director, President Sherwood, then in his fiftieth year of service with the Old Bay Line, deciding to decline this appointment in favor of a younger man. "Captain" Sherwood resigned on October 23, and although Mr. S. Davis Warfield was elected president, he did not exercise that office until the war was over and the government returned the railroads and ship lines to their owners.

It will be recalled that the menace of German submarines was such that inhabitants of the Atlantic seaboard managed to develop a good case of jitters. The War Department was especially concerned with the numerous strategic points of military and naval significance surrounding the Hampton Roads area and in March, 1918, a submarine net was strung between Forts Monroe and Wool to block the chance entrance into the Roads of enemy undersea craft and a second net off Thimble Shoals was placed a few months later. These were only opened for brief periods during the day to let ships in and out and naturally the Bay steamers' schedules had to be adjusted so that their movements would conform. The majority of Chesapeake mariners felt that the nets only served as an unmitigated nuisance and that their value as defence was nil.

It is no secret that under Federal operation, all American transportation systems suffered tremendous depreciation. As far as the Bay steamship lines were concerned, the boats were permitted to get out of condition and the scrub brush was used as sparingly as possible and the paint brush not at all.

During this demoralized period disaster came to one of the Old Bay Line's steamers which the government was operating. On the night of May 24, 1919, the *Virginia*[II] caught fire and became a total loss. The ship was crowded with passengers bound for Newport News to welcome returning troop transports from overseas, many of whom did not even have time to grab their clothes before abandoning the steamer. The *Florida, City of Norfolk,* and *City of Annapolis* hastened to the scene of the accident and picked up the survivors. Of the disaster, Mr. Compton the Federal Director said:*

> Too much praise cannot be given Captain Walter G. Lane of the *Virginia.* He stayed by his ship till every soul was off despite the fact that his hands were burned and he was suffering great pain.

Despite the fact that he was in no way personally responsible for the unfortunate event and had handled the situation with rare judgment and skill, it is said that Captain Lane never completely got over the disaster and retired from the sea the following year a very much disheartened man.

Even though the National Railroad Administration was in charge, the Old Bay Line inherited a black eye for which it was hardly responsible. It is true that the same Bay Line officers commanded the ships for the Federal Authorities, but as the war period was characterized by labor troubles all over the country, it was

---

*Baltimore *Sun,* May 25, 1919, pp. 16, 6, 7.

impossible to maintain the willing and well disciplined crews for which the Chesapeake has long been famous.

It was some time after the Armistice before the government returned their property to the railroads and not until March 1, 1920, that the occupation officially terminated and the Old Bay Line resumed its own management.

The Line's History Brought Up to Date

CHAPTER X

HERE is some consolation in numbers and at the end of the war the Old Bay Line was not alone in being faced with critical times. Added to the fact that its equipment was almost hopelessly out of condition, the general nation-wide slump was not conducive to an immediate rehabilitation of the shipping business. The Chesapeake Line, not having lost one of its most important units, was in far better condition even though its status was far from enviable. In 1920 then, the Old Bay Line's fleet numbered the following venerable craft: passenger steamers *Alabama*[II], twenty-seven years old, and *Florida*[II], thirteen years old; freighters *Gaston,* thirty-nine years old, and *Raleigh,* fourteen years old; and the tug *Elsie,* twenty-seven years old.

In the operation of daily over-night service the ownership of at least three passenger steamers is to be desired, for in case of accident or merely periodic overhaul, the third vessel is needed to replace the regulars on the line. Not only did the Old Bay Line not have that necessary third vessel, but the condition of the *Alabama* was critical in that she required immediate boiler replacement. Suitable vessels to fill in an established service are not to be easily located and the Old Bay Line had to make out as best it could through the winter of 1920-1921 with the *Benjamin B. Odell* chartered from the Central Hudson Steamboat Company. Had it been a heavy winter, the *Odell* could not have been used at all for she was of the excursion type suitable only for what she was designed, namely operating on the protected Hudson River in summertime.

Further reviewing of their equipment determined the sale in

October, 1920, of their old freighter *Gaston* to the Gulfport (Mississippi) Fruit and Steamship Company. The *Gaston* needed considerable repairs and as their other cargo boat, the *Raleigh*[II], was sufficient for handling the all too small amount of freight, the move was a sensible one. The *Gaston* served various owners, mostly located in the Gulf of Mexico, until dropped from the Register in 1935 in her fifty-fourth year.

In order to recapture the former standards of service and efficiency in its passenger department, the Old Bay Line appointed a "Director of Service" on January 1, 1921. The announcement of this appointment frankly stated that due to the "demoralization of service incident to Federal Control, . . . the accommodations offered to the traveling public on Bay steamers became unattractive and untrustworthy."*

The biggest move was still to come, however, and in 1922 President Warfield announced an extensive program of replacement for both the Seaboard Railway and the Old Bay Line. To effect this replacement, a new corporation, the Seaboard-Bay Line Company, was organized *pro tem* to make possible the obtaining of new rolling stock for the railroad and new steamers for the Bay Line. With the means for acquiring modern ships in sight, coupled with a further extension of the Baltimore Steam Packet Company's charter by the Maryland General Assembly giving the right of perpetual succession, the outlook was considerably brightened.

The same year contracts were awarded to the Pusey and Jones Corporation of Wilmington, Delaware, for the construction of the new and identical ships *State of Maryland*[II] and *State of Virginia*[II]. Like the Chesapeake Line boats of 1911, the new Old Bay liners would have three passenger decks but were to be considerably larger and were designed to carry 700 tons of freight and a maximum of 600 passengers. Looking back along the years, it will be remembered that when the Line began operation in 1840, their

---

*Baltimore *Sun*, Dec. 28, 1920, p. 16.

—*Courtesy of Pusey & Jones Corp.*

The *State of Maryland* on her trial trip, December, 1922.

little *Jewess* could only carry 75 passengers "comfortably" and that the side-wheel *Virginia*[I] coming out in 1879 had room for 300.

In the new steamers the dining rooms seating 100 people were lifted from the hold and placed on the after end of the main deck where passengers were afforded a view of Chesapeake Bay while enjoying their meals. The saloons were fitted out in Colonial style and gave a cool and comfortable appearance and there were also glass-enclosed music rooms on the gallery decks.

—*Courtesy of Pusey & Jones Corp.*

The *State of Virginia*, delivered to the Old Bay Line in February, 1923.

It is significant to note that in size and power, the engines of the new boats, although of improved balance, duplicated the machinery installed in the *Alabama* thirty years before. This may at first seem strange, but reviewing the history of the steamboat on Chesapeake Bay it will be recalled that to all intents and purposes the need for increased speed disappeared when the successors to the little *Virginia,* which took 24 hours to make the trip in 1819, had perfected their machinery to the point where the time was cut.in half. Its evening meal was one of the big drawing cards for the Old Bay Line and this would be lost if departures were postponed till late at night. To apply a reduction on the other end would be equally profitless, for to arrive in the very early morning would be of no conceivable advantage since the debarkation of freight and passengers would have to wait for daylight anyway. Although capable of covering the run·in considerably less time, the Old Bay Line had been and still is operating on a twelve-hour schedule and their reserve of speed is only of use in case of delays before starting or on route, and a further reserve would be both unnecessary and expensive.

The keel of the first of the new steamers, the *State of Maryland,* was laid on March 4, 1922, and she was launched with appropriate ceremonies on July 25, making her maiden voyage down to Norfolk on January 8, 1923, commanded by Captain W. C. Almy and with J. L. Marshall, her present captain, as first mate. The *State of Virginia* followed close on her heels, being launched on September 6, 1922, and joining the line under the command of Captain R. S. Foster in February of the next year, less than a month after the *State of Maryland* had commenced service.

As before, when new ships were put in commission, the Old Bay Line disposed of its old ones. In this case the *Alabama,* although considerably older than the *Florida,* was retained as the spare boat of the line and the latter was sold in January, 1924, to the Monticello Steamship Company. This organization had looked afar for its new vessel, for it operated a line of ferry steamers on San Francisco Bay.

The *Florida* was boxed in and otherwise prepared for the lengthy voyage to the West Coast via Panama under her own steam. The trip out during the Summer of 1924 was long but uneventful and on arrival the *Florida* was rebuilt as a double-ended ferry at Vallejo and, renamed *Calistoga,* entered service on October 11 of the same year. Later on a merger of the various San Francisco Bay ferry lines took place and the *Calistoga* was acquired by the Southern Pacific Golden Gate Ferries Ltd. According to the latest reports, this company still owns her, although she is at present tied up await-ing a purchaser since the new Bay bridges have been instrumental in closing down most of the San Francisco ferry lines.

The same month the *Florida* was sold, a purchaser appeared for the *Raleigh.* With the enormous increase in freight space afforded by the new steamers, the Old Bay Line, for the first time in many years, had no need for a vessel designed to handle cargo only and the *Raleigh*[II] was sold to the Saginaw and Bay City (Michigan) Steamship Company and taken to the Great Lakes. She came back to the Atlantic Seaboard in 1929 as the *Marion* owned by the Colon-ial Navigation Company, operating on Long Island Sound. In 1938 she was acquired by Philippine interests and taken out across the Pacific.

Further changes in the fleet consisted in exchanging the tug *Elsie* for an even older vessel, the iron-hull *Mary O'Riorden,* which had been built in Buffalo during the War of Secession. Despite her age, the new tug was both larger and in better condition than the *Elsie,* although the Bay Line did not hold on to her for long, deciding in 1927 to give up entirely the ownership of tugs and to charter them when needed instead. Today the diesel tug *Hustler* of the H. T. Corporation is used for undocking the steamers at Baltimore, barge movements, and so forth.

When the new steamers had been conceived it had been decided to build three of them to identical plans. On August 22, 1927, the third contract was awarded to the Pusey and Jones Corporation and the new vessel began to take form. Less than two months later President S. Davies Warfield died and inasmuch as he had worked

The *President Warfield* alongside at Old Point Comfort. From a photograph by the author taken from the Hotel Chamberlin roof.

so hard and successfully in putting the Old Bay Line back on its feet again, it was decided to name the new boat *President Warfield* in his memory.

Mr. Legh R. Powell, Jr., the present incumbent, was elevated to the presidency of the Bay Line and Seaboard Railway shortly thereafter and has wisely guided the policies of the Line since 1927, Mr. Robert E. Dunn, vice-president and present operating head of the line, joining him in 1934.

Although identical in plan to her sister-ships, the *President Warfield,* flag-ship of the Line, was given a few minor alterations and additions suggested in the operation of the other steamers, and for this reason her gross tonnage is computed at 1,814 tons as opposed to 1,783 in the other boats. All three were built of steel, the plating of which carried up one deck higher than on other steamers in operation on the Chesapeake. Likewise, although all three were originally coal burning, the *President Warfield* and *State of Maryland* were converted to the use of oil fuel in 1933 by the installation of Todd

—Courtesy of Mr. P. S. Gornto.

The *President Warfield* at the Company's pier, Norfolk, 1939.

oil burners by the Maryland Dry Dock Company, the *State of Virginia* received a similar installation in 1939.

The addition of the *President Warfield* to the line marked the termination of the *Alabama's* useful thirty-five-year career on the Chesapeake. Like the *Florida,* the *Alabama* found a purchaser on the West Coast and she, too, made the long trip out by the Panama Canal in the Summer of 1928. On arrival she was converted to a car ferry by her new owners, the Progress Improvement Company of Seattle, Washington. As the *City of Victoria* she was operated between Everett, Washington, and Victoria, British Columbia, and only a short time ago was purchased by the Puget Sound Bridge and Dredging Company, contractor for Alaska's, $3,000,000 naval air base construction. Her new owners have towed her to Sitka, where she is now used as a floating hotel for about half of the 500 construction workers. When this job is finished undoubtedly the shipwrecker's torch and hammer will claim her and a long and useful career will be brought to an end.

Events in the past decade of the Old Bay Line's history are so clearly in mind that we will not attempt more than sketching them in as briefly as possible. In 1928 Captain Almy was given command of the latest ship, Captain Foster took over the *State of Maryland,* and the *State of Virginia* became the spare boat of the line. Alternating, both the latter and the *President Warfield* were chartered for the Summers of 1929, 1930, and 1931 and ran on Long Island Sound with both the Colonial Line and the Eastern Steamship Company's Boston to New York service. It was decided later to keep all three boats in the Chesapeake, since the spare vessel could earn more running local excursions and by chartering it, the Line might find that it was absent at a time that it might be most needed.

An unfortunate happening occurred on August 3, 1932, when the *State of Maryland* ran down and sank the watermelon schooner *Milton S. Lankford* off the mouth of the Potomac River. Since the schooner was carrying no lights visible to the steamer, the accident could hardly have been avoided. Another collision occurred on July 14, 1936, when, for no accountable reason, the steamer *Golden Harvest* rammed the *State of Virginia* as the latter was returning from an excursion with Governor Harry W. Nice and 263 passengers aboard. Although shipyard workers had to burn off the bow of the *Golden Harvest* with acetylene torches to get the vessels apart, no one was injured in the mishap and the *State of Virginia* was easily repaired again as good as new.

In addition to the all-too-many troubles inherited by the Old Bay Line from the National Railroad Administration, one, namely that of prohibition, has not been considered. No longer were the appetites of Bay Line passengers to be whetted by a tall mint julep and what meal is there that might not be improved by a gentle libation beforehand! More serious, however, was the smuggling and transportation of liquor on Old Bay Line steamers. Although the company made every effort to comply with the law, for a time during this incredible era occasional bootleg shipments brought on board from foreign ships at Hampton Roads made up cargoes not appearing on the manifests.

As stated, the Company did its level best to coöperate with the Coast Guard to prevent liquor getting aboard and for his reason Bay Line officials were highly insensed when one March night in 1929, a Coast Guard cutter fired a shot across the *President Warfield's* bow and ordered her to heave-to for examination. President Powell justly expressed his indignation for this highhanded procedure and the Coast Guard itself was not at all in sympathy with the action of the master of this particular cutter. Captain P. H. Scott, commandant of the Norfolk Coast Guard station stated* that it was "unthinkable that a passenger steamer should be stopped. . . . as if she were trying to escape" and criticized his subordinate for not postponing examination until the steamer docked, at which time, of course, he would have had the Bay Line people's every assistance. Although the Bay Line's years had spanned four wars, this marked the first occasion when one of their ships was fired on. Happily prohibition is now a thing of the past and today the steamers have well patronized cocktail decks open to the sky in Summer, and cozy tap-rooms in Winter.

The Winter of 1934 was a repetition of the severe ice condition of 1917 and both Bay lines were forced to give up occasional sailings. The Chesapeake Line *City of Norfolk* had to be put in dry dock at Newport News to secure shell plates damaged by ice floes. The August before, both lines experienced varying amounts of damage when a freak hurricane struck the Chesapeake area. The *State of Maryland* managed to come through with the loss of only a few lifeboat covers and some broken crockery. The storm was so unusual, however, that it will be recounted in more detail in the following chapter.

During the Summer of 1935, the *State of Virginia* was again chartered to the Colonial Navigation Company, but the following

---

*Baltimore *Sun,* March 10, 1929, p. 3.

year the management decided to employ her regularly during the warm months in "house-boat" cruises from Baltimore to Ocean View, a popular Virginia seaside resort, and to Yorktown to afford passengers an opportunity of visiting Colonial Williamsburg. Practically all American ship lines used their vessels for cruises when occasion offered and the Old Bay Line found this new venture to be well patronized. The schedule of these cruises called for sailings of the *State of Virginia* from Baltimore on Friday evenings and she would anchor off Ocean View for one night, passengers using the boat as a hotel. A 25-foot launch, the *Marguerite,* was acquired in May 1936 for use as ship-to-shore tender.

Another, and year-round, business developed by the Line after the war consisted in attracting Florida-bound and other motorists to use the steamers instead of a hotel and thus shorten their driving by eliminating 230 miles of crowded roads and placing them in the heart of Virginia's many historic shrines. When the automobile first began to be considered as competition to the steamboat, lines all over the country were scornful and attempted to ignore them. Motorists were not wanted. They had to pay heavy freight charges and were subjected to all sorts of annoyances imposed by underwriters such as draining gasoline from the tanks, etc.* As much as anything, the Depression and resultant unfilled cargo space brought ship owners to their senses and they realized that since the automobile tourist was here to stay that they had better do all that was possible to gain a patronage that they would otherwise miss entirely. The Old Bay Line was a pioneer in recognizing this trend and many a sound dollar has been earned by luring the motorist off the road and giving him a good night's sleep on board a Bay Line steamer.

Still another vessel was added to the Line in 1936 when they acquired the *Alcyone,* once an elegant Lawley-built auxiliary steam yacht, since converted to a cargo boat. The *Alcyone* was purchased at rock bottom price and after spending some money in fixing her

---

*An Old Bay Line circular issued in 1917 stated: "Automobiles propelled by gasoline will not be received for transportation unless tanks are empty and thoroughly dry."

In the Pilot House of the *State of Virginia*, 1923. Left to right, First Officer J. R. Hudgins, Captain R. S. Foster, and Quartermaster C. S. Cannon at the wheel.

Chief Engineer George M. Johnson in the Engine Room of the *State of Virginia*, 1923.

up, the Old Bay Line had at its disposal a substantial diesel-electric freighter available for charter or to use in transporting special freight shipments.

Merely to present a comparison in prices, it is interesting to observe that a modern steel barge costing $8,000 built for the Company by the Old Dominion Railroad Corporation in 1936 cost exactly the same amount as had their passenger steamer *Pocahontas* in 1840. The length of the contract covering the construction of this barge is further evidence of how, during the past century, life has become increasingly complicated, for in 1840 a memorandum scratched across the back of an envelope would have sufficed for a fleet of barges.

The decade spanned in this chapter saw the termination of two famous old steamboat lines brought on by a variety of economic causes happily not affecting the Old Bay Line. In 1932 the Champlain Transportation Company, then the oldest steamboat line in the world, abandoned its night-boat service running the length of Lake Champlain, and a ferry boat concern which now operates a Summer ten-mile automobile ferry across the lake acquired the property in 1937. With more nostalgia than accuracy, the ferry still advertises itself as the oldest steamboat line in the country but, inasmuch as the Champlain Transportation Company's name no longer is included in the current *Official Guide of the Railways and Steam Navigation Lines of the United States,* it is an unfortunate but accepted fact that its end has arrived.

Only seven years younger than the Old Bay Line, the famous Fall River Line previously noted in these pages, wound up its affairs on July 27, 1937, in the ninety-first year of operation, and the side-wheelers *Priscilla, Commonwealth,* and *Providence* have since been converted to scrap. The Fall River Line might have survived as an independent organization, but in the attempt to get the New York, New Haven, and Hartford Railroad back onto its feet the famous old line received shock after shock until a sit-down strike proved more than it could carry and its doom was sealed.

However, the Old Bay Line, well grounded from the first, had survived previous depressions and is today in a strong position that well brooks the supposition that its second century of operation will be an equally successful one.

Although not brand new, its fleet of steamers has been kept in the best of condition and constantly modernized by the addition of the latest improvements affecting comfort and seaworthiness. In 1938, Grinnell sprinkler systems were installed throughout and during the Summer of last year, the steamers were given radio direction-finders and ship-to-shore radio telephones, and thus again scored a first for steamboat lines on Chesapeake Bay. All three boats have a social directress and of course passengers are afforded a complete line of deck sports. At the present writing Captain R. S. Foster is master of the *President Warfield* and Captain J. L. Marshall of the *State of Maryland*. Captain P. L. Parker commands the *State of Virginia* on excursions and J. W. Gresham, the *Alcyone*. The diesel tug *Hustler* is chartered at Baltimore and a large fleet of covered barges owned by the company are located at both terminal ports.

The Chesapeake Line, originally operating on the York River only, as we have seen, has maintained in addition sailings parallel to the Old Bay Line since 1896. Today, however, their York River business has diminished to the point where one steamer two or three times weekly is sufficient. On the Baltimore-Norfolk route, their new ships, the *City of Baltimore* and *City of Norfolk,* coming out in 1911 gave them a decided advantage until 1923 when the Old Bay Line provided their new vessels for the service. The Chesapeake Line was operating the old *Columbia,* rival of the *Virginia*[II] in 1907 for the Jamestown Exposition traffic, and the *City of Richmond* on their York River Line until 1923 when the former was converted to a freighter and renamed *City of Atlanta.* A Newport News-built passenger steamer, named *Yorktown,* was added for this service in 1928, the same year that the Bay Line launched the *President Warfield.*

A serious set-back to the Chesapeake Line occurred on July 29, 1937, when a fire of undetermined origin broke out on the *City of Baltimore* and she burned to the waterline causing three casualties. Since that time they have used the comparatively new *Yorktown* and the 29-year-old *City of Norfolk* on the run paralleling the Old Bay Line, reserving the *City of Richmond* for the York River. They also own a little wooden hulled tug, the *Southern,* built in 1905.

The foregoing thumb-nail sketch of the Chesapeake Line and its present fleet is presented as background to the announcement that an agreement has been reached whereby the Old Bay Line is to purchase the property and assets of its rival. It is quite natural that a purchase of this character involving far-flung financial and legal interests is not only a complicated but also a lengthy procedure.* That the move is a sensible one is proven by the fact that it has long been obvious that, except during peak seasons, one line could more than adequately handle the Baltimore-Norfolk trade. During the height of the Depression it was ridiculous for two more than half-empty steamers to be maintaining a parallel service. In the new combine the Old Bay Line will take over the property and good will of the Chesapeake Steamship Company and although obviously some of the steamers will be disposed of, the resultant service will prove more efficient for all ports of call. Normal competition is healthy for any business. There comes a time, however, when if carried too far the result would provide inefficient service from both competitors. The result of this acquisition will be far-reaching and the Old Bay Line will be even better enabled to meet the real and increasing competition from the motorbuses and trucks.

The question naturally arises as to why the Old Bay Line should be absorbing the Chesapeake Line and not *vice versa*. Certainly there are more reasons beyond the fact that at present the Old Bay Line owns the more modern fleet. These other reasons, intangible in themselves, may be best summed up in the vision and foresight of

---

*See Norfolk *Virginian-Pilot,* April 17, 1940, pp. 15, 20, for financial details of the contemplated purchase.

those pioneers who, a century ago, determined to give the public a steamboat line that invariably offered the best service available, a tradition which has been faithfully upheld by their successors down to the present day.

Storm on the Bay

CHAPTER XI

IMPASSIONED writers describing the great bay of the Chesapeake dwell at length on its calm, pellucid waters and its balmy, sun-drenched shores. Although undoubtedly the Chesapeake has more than its fair share of clement weather, nevertheless when on rare occasions howling winter Nor-easters sweep down the Bay and growling ice-packs choke its river mouths, it is decidedly more comfortable in a chair by the fire at home than in the pilot house of a steamer feeling her way cautiously through the murk.

However, two steamers of the Old Bay Line nightly leave their terminal ports of Baltimore and Norfolk in fair weather or foul. Their captains learn to expect fogs and snow squalls in winter, increased vigilance is called for, but regardless of weather, Chesapeake ship-masters seldom fail to make scheduled time.

Not all bad weather is reserved for winter though and let us assume that on the evening of August 22, 1933, we had boarded the *State of Maryland*[II], Captain John L. Marshall commanding, for the southbound trip to Norfolk.

There is no place here to dwell at length on the peculiarities of those storms rightfully most dreaded by mariners—tropical hurricanes. Suffice if to say that these often appallingly violent disturbances which skirt our southern seaboard States usually swing out off-shore below Cape Hatteras following the path of the Gulf Stream to dissipate themselves in mid-Atlantic. Occasionally they do not, however, and New England will long remember what happened in 1938 when one of these freak West India hurricanes played havoc along its shores. Fortunately this storm passed by the Chesapeake area, but we are now in 1933 and this time the Bay had not been so fortunate. Old residents called "the August storm" the worst that ever wracked its normally hospitable coast.

—*Courtesy The Old Bay Line.*

The *State of Maryland*. Built in 1923, by Pusey & Jones Corp.
(After a contemporary painting by Bishop.)

As is well known, the general form of a hurricane is circular with winds sweeping around and converging on a calm spot of abnormally low pressure in the very center or axis of the storm— like a giant whirlpool of air. In the West India variety this center itself is in motion traveling northward in a great arc at a relatively. slow speed. Not so the raging blasts which surround it: meteorologists have measured speeds sometimes well in excess of 100 miles an hour. Since the winds are circling the center low pressure area which is itself in motion, both the direction of the wind and its force will vary in relation to one's position to the storm track. Thus in the regions frequented by hurricanes it is possible for the experienced mariner to plot in advance the path the storm will take and if he is off shore with plenty of sea-room, he may be able to get out of its track entirely. It is the center of a hurricane which is most dreaded.

It was dark and blustery the August night that the *State of Maryland* had sailed from Baltimore and north-east storm warnings were flying at the staff surmounting the American Building. Earlier Weather Bureau reports had of course noted that a hurricane was sweeping up the coast, but since its normal path would take it out to sea, shipping in Baltimore went about its usual business considering a stiff Nor-easter the normal corrillary to disturbed conditions off shore. At six-thirty promptly the *State of Maryland's* deep-throated steam whistle blared, the tug came alongside, stretched taut her stern line and as she backed out of her slip helped to swing her around in the narrow basin. Under way and gingerly steaming along the lane of flashing buoys that marked the channel, the *State of Maryland* headed down the Patapsco for the open Bay. Twilight was short, and with the gusty wind striking the ship on her port quarter, she leaned slightly as she encountered choppier water as the river widened near its mouth. At a comfortably safe distance behind, the gleaming running lights shining emerald and ruby marked the position of the Chesapeake Line steamer *City of Norfolk,* Captain Edward James, likewise Norfolk bound and following the same track down the Bay.

Despite the rolling of the steamer and the blustery wind on deck, it was comfortable and cozy in the saloon of the *State of Maryland,* and dinner completed, her passengers went about their usual business of amusing themselves until bed time. Horse racing and other games claimed their devotees in the palm room on the galley deck; others read, wrote, or chatted in the saloon; while still others ensconsed in the comfortable leather chairs in the social hall below on the main deck aft sipped their tall glasses and argued on the evils of prohibition. Watchmen made their ceaseless rounds; stewards and pantrymen put away the dishes and straightened the dining saloon against the morrow's breakfast; down below engineers and water-tenders hovered over their pulsing machines; and in the pilot house the second mate on watch peered intently out through the "middle window" and gave muted instructions to his quartermaster for now half a spoke right rudder, now steady as you go. The lookout, collar turned up, had wedged himself by the rail at the bow and occasionally ducked to dodge a dose of spray sweeping across the fore deck. Four bells rang. All snug and running smoothly, the ship settled down to her normal nightly routine as Captain Marshall having taken his customary last look around closed the door between his quarters and the pilot house and turned in. Fate had decreed that his night's rest was not to be an unbroken one.

A violent lurch almost threw him from his bunk. Jumping out and quickly dressing, he glanced at the clock screwed to the bulk-head above his desk. Two A. M. In another moment he was in the pilot house. Conditions were different from when he had gone to bed.

The barometer four hours before had been normal, now the pointer was dropping rapidly, as wind and sea increased. The wind was blowing gale force from the north-east. The steamer's stern would rise to waves dashing up behind as the bow buried itself deep into the smother while the ship seemed to gather herself together for a yawing rush down the wind. Rolling and careening she plowed on into the night.

Anxiety could be read in every face in that darkened pilot house. What was the best course to follow? The safety of a hundred people lay in the judgment of the *Maryland's* captain. Even though the ship was laboring, rolling her guards well under in the troughs of those sickly seas, she must and would keep on. Intermediate ports of refuge could not be considered. Disaster would have certainly come to him who tried blindly to bring his ship into a river such as the Rappahannock for shelter, for by now the wind had swung more to the eastward and the only possible havens lay along a dreaded lee shore.

On such a night as this, the shipmaster has to face his fate alone. Behind on the *City of Norfolk* an experienced captain doubted that his ship could live in such raging seas. He had kept her up to the eastward hoping to break the force of the swell by getting a lee under Maryland's Eastern Shore. Edging her in towards Pocomoke Sound closer than he dared, the Chesapeake Line ship ran hard aground near Watts Island. Providentially she held together and abandonment was unnecessary. It was some time before her people could be gotten off ashore, but despite the fact that the ship remained aground for several days, she suffered only minor damage and no one was hurt.

Meanwhile the strongly built *State of Maryland* was holding her course. Lighthouses and buoys which normally would have guided her were obscured in the raging night. Taking into consideration the drift caused by that terrific wind her captain unerringly held her on her course by dead-reckoning, guided by that uncanny sixth sense which is the seaman's heritage. It was too hazardous to attempt to turn the ship around and heave to. Her salvation depended in her being able to withstand the punishment of driving on southward, and reaching port before the storm center engulfed her. To delay would only prolong the danger and the agony of suspense. With confidence in his ship and crew, the captain kept her throbbing engine full ahead and only slowed down in the blinding squalls.

Torrents of rain drove against the pilot house windows obliterating vision. At times even the flag-staff on the bow momentarily disappeared from view. Sea and sky were fused into one aqueous element that relentlessly tore at the ship, bent on her distruction. The noise of screaming wind and smashing wave was deafening. Sailors detailed to put extra lashings to secure objects on deck had their breath beaten back when they faced the blast and cupping their mouths and shouting they could not be heard by their fellows only a few feet away.

Below was a shambles. Freight loose in the hold, crockery smashed, chairs and tables upturned and sliding around the cabins. Naturally few passengers preferred to remain in their bunks and a solemn and dejected group assembled in the saloon as the steamer cavorted, groaned and twisted beneath them. No complaints were voiced, however, for all felt that the ship was fighting a gallant fight and her company doing their best to aid her.

On she lunged through the darkness. By now the wind had increased from a roar to a shriek. Lifeboat covers were bodily ripped off and sent scudding down to leeward. The guy wires supporting the tall funnel sang like tightened bow-strings. Ropes beat a continuous tattoo against their staffs while all around the short steep seas crashed and raged. Convulsive shivers ran through the ship as unrelenting waves smashed into her stern. She could take this punishment for a while, but what if it got worse?

Meanwhile the barometer continued its headlong descent. Squalls of hurricane force followed each other without break. The watch in the pilot house peered intently forward for some landmark to guide them. A momentary lull and a beacon loomed up to starboard. It was comforting to know that she was still on her course. Then gradually dawn came, while black night thinned out to gray morning. Thimble Shoals lay to leeward and it would not be long before the ship could turn down to the westward towards the mouth of Hampton Roads. A lee would be found under Old Point Comfort and the captain decided to try to make the dock. Fate decreed otherwise. As the *State of Maryland* tried to swing around, the wind caught her broadside and all the power of the engines and her rudder would not suffice to drive her into the wind. Back she swung bound for the Elizabeth River and a haven at last. Waves were breaking clean across the Old Point wharf.

Hearts were lighter with the goal in sight and even though the wind still raged with unabated fury, the seas were lower in the more protected water. Along the shore the steamer's officers could see the remains of small craft thrown up on land and smashed to matchwood. Trees uprooted, houses blown down, all gave mute evidence of what the night had experienced. Lambert's Point was left astern, then Pinner's Point and now the pier itself loomed up through the flying scud.

It took almost an hour for Captain Marshall to bring the *State of Maryland* alongside. The wharf was flooded and only the tops of the bollards to tie up to were visible. Rowboats ferried ashore those of her passengers who had to leave immediately, but with the lower part of town inundated many preferred the safe haven of the ship itself which had so gallantly fought it out in that raging night and won.

Their thankfulness took form in a resolution of gratitude to the ship and her master. It was just luck he said, but those who know the Chesapeake and her mariners realize that to come out on top, luck must be combined with the years of training and skill that go into the knowledge of their business.

JOHN M. ROBINSON
President 1867-1893

R. C. HOFFMAN
President 1893-1899

J. S. WILLIAMS
President 1899-1904

JOHN R. SHERWOOD
President 1907-1918

S. DAVIES WARFIELD
President 1918-1927

SOME FORMER PRESIDENTS OF THE BALTIMORE
STEAM PACKET COMPANY

Personalities in the Bay Line's History

CHAPTER XII

IN an attempt in the preceding pages to adequately cover events in the history of the Old Bay Line's first century, we have been conscious of the fact that for the most part little or nothing has been said of the men who ran the ships and of the passengers they carried. Particularly for the early years of operation of the line is it difficult to find out about the people themselves. A few names have been handed down in contemporary documents, but in essence these are merely just so many letters strung together, and even an attempt to locate portraits of some prominent men in the organization as for example of Andrew F. Henderson, the first president, have been to no avail.

In the matter of passengers who traveled via Old Bay Line source materials are even more elusive. We can be sure, however, that a representative cross-section of American life could have been found at some time or another on a Bay Line ship. This would run the entire gamut from Presidents of the United States down to the lowliest citizens. Only rarely have travelers committed memoirs of their experiences on the Bay Line to writing, and then, with foreign visitors, it was as equally often to blame as to praise. Tyrone Power mentioned the Yankee peddlers; Lieutenant DeRoos, the well-dressed and "beautiful" passengers. That socially prominent and otherwise important people took the Bay Line is evidenced by the constant improvements made to the boats and a progressive elevating of the standards of travel.

A cross-section of American life: men, women, and children; old and young, rich and poor, happy and care-worn, in love and disillus-

ioned, well and ill; traveling for business and pleasure; going on
vacations and to war. These then are the people who have trod the
Bay Line's gangplanks for the past one hundred years.

Captain Edward Trippe was Chesapeake Bay's first steamboat
master. It will be recalled that in conjunction with two men who
were later to feature prominently in the beginnings of the Baltimore
Steam Packet Company, he was instrumental in having built, in
1813, the first successful steamboat on the body of water from which
she took her name: the *Chesapeake*. Captain Trippe later commanded the *Philadelphia* and the *United States,* all of which were
used in the upper Bay between Baltimore and Frenchtown.

The Ferguson family also contributed several members to the
steamboat fraternity. Captain John Ferguson having gained his
training in sailing packets on the Norfolk run, commanded the *Virginia* when she came out in 1817. Benjamin Ferguson owned both
the *Virginia* and the *Norfolk* until sold by his estate in 1828 to mark
the beginning of the Maryland and Virginia Steam Boat Company.
James Ferguson was agent for this organization in 1835 and held this
post for the Old Bay Line in Norfolk as late as 1851.

Captain Moses Rogers, having made the very first ocean passage
in a steamer when he took the *Phoenix* from New York to the
Delaware in 1807, brought the little *Eagle* down to the Chesapeake
in 1815 and blazed the route by steam from Norfolk to Baltimore.
The following year he likewise "imported" the *New Jersey,* but it is
in his capacity as master of the famous transatlantic auxiliary *Savannah* in 1819 that he will be long remembered as a pioneer exponent
of the art of steam navigation.

Of other early Chesapeake steamboat masters only their names
have survived: Capt. John Campbell of the *Norfolk* in 1819; Capt.
Daniel W. Crocker of the "swift and elegant" *Petersburg;* Capt.
Coffin of the *Powhatan;* Capt. Middleton of the *Roanoke;* all saw
service prior to 1820.

In the second decade of steamboat operation on the Chesapeake
the names of the following mariners appear: Capt. Brown, relief

captain of both the *Virginia* and *Norfolk;* Captain William Owen of the latter vessel; Captain Chapman of the *Petersburg* and later *Patrick Henry* on the James; and Captain George Weems who owned the *Eagle* and introduced steam navigation to the Patuxent River.

Captain William Rollins, a redoubtable mariner, first appears as master of the *Governor Walcott* on the upper Bay in 1830, but shortly thereafter he was in turn to command the *Virginia* then running between Baltimore, Norfolk and Charleston, and the *Georgia*[I] whose construction he superintended for the Atlantic Line. As previously mentioned, Captain Rollins went further south when the

CAPTAIN JAMES CANNON
Master of Old Bay Line steamboats during the Company's
first 28 years.

Old Bay Line took over in 1840 and during the Mexican War he commanded the United States steamship *Neptune* and later the "magnificent" *Isabel*. At the time of his death in 1877 in his seventy-second year, Captain Rollins was mentioned as the oldest commander of steam vessels, counting years of service, in the United States, and he had long been recognized as one of the best pilots on the South Atlantic coast.

We have listed the names of the incorporators of the Old Bay Line when it made its bow in 1840. The following served the company as its first shipmasters: James Cannon, James Coffey, George W. Russell, and Thomas Sutton.

Captain Cannon commanded the little *Pocahontas* in 1836, was first mate of the *Herald* when she came out in 1842, commanded the *Georgia* in 1849, and later the *North Carolina*. He was on the *North Carolina* on her ill-fated voyage in 1859 and transferred to the *Adelaide* until his resignation in 1868, having then been with the Old Bay Line for the first 28 years of its existence.

Captain Coffey was with the Atlantic Line as master of the *South Carolina* in 1836, and then took the *Georgia* for the Bay Line from 1840 until he was succeeded by Captain Cannon. Captain Russell is first heard of as master of the Talbot Line *Paul Jones* in 1838 where he earned the "reputation for care and ability." He took over the *Jewess* when the Old Bay Line started and served on all of the first boats of the company until in 1854 he was assigned to the new *Louisiana,* and received the gift of a silver speaking trumpet from his many friends at the south end of the Bay. He was still in command of the *Louisiana* at the time of the *Great Eastern's* visit in 1860, and after the War was given the new iron steamer *Thomas Kelso* when she came out in 1866.

Captain Sutton, another doughty mariner, took command of the *Alabama* in 1838 and joined the Bay Line as master of the *South Carolina*. He was badly injured when the *Medora* exploded on her trial trip, but as soon as he had recovered the company gave him command of the *Jewess*. He was also master of the *Herald* for a while and the last mention of his name in connection with the Old Bay Line occurred in 1851 when he was back in charge of the *Jewess* again.

Other early Bay Line captains whose names appear briefly on the record are Captain James Holmes of the *Jewess* in 1840, Captain Hardie of the *Herald* in 1852, and Captain Pearson of the *Georgia* in 1859. All had previously been connected with the old Maryland and Virginia Steam Boat Company, the former on the *Kentucky* and the latter on the *Norfolk*. A Captain Parrish commanded the *Vir-*

ginia prior to the Old Bay Line's inception when she was trading along the Eastern Shore.

In early times it was customary to include the names of ships together with their captains with all advertisements. Following the War of Secession this practice seems to have been gradually abandoned and today short-run sound and coastwise steamship companies rarely even mention the names of their vessels in advertisements when in regular service. This trend is a natural one for with the standardization of steamship lines and the operation of virtually identical ships, the personality of an individual boat becomes submerged and there are many Old Bay Line passengers who make the over-night trip without even knowing either their ship's or her captain's names. When steamers first made their appearance on the waters of the Chesapeake, the rôle of shipmaster was slightly different from today. Then captains were hosts and passengers their guests, a custom proven by the fact that on the *Surprise* in the 1820's, Captain George Stiles provided his passengers with solid silver service in the dining saloon.

In the post-war period, Captain Darius J. Hill, termed "one of the most popular gentlemen ever known to the traveling public" first appears as master of the *Georgeanna* in 1866. He commanded the *Louisiana* for a short time and when the new *Florida* came out ten years later he was stationed at the "middle window" of her pilot house. Later he was to serve the Old Bay Line in the capacity of superintendent, being mentioned as holding this position as late as 1892 when his long and useful career terminated.

Still·other post-war Old Bay Line shipmasters included Captain A. K. Cralle of the *Thomas Kelso,* the *New Jersey,* and as late as 1877 of the freighter *Seaboard.* At this time Captain P. McCarrick commanded the *Eolus* and, during and after the war Captain Thomas Edgar, first of three generations of Bay Line employees, the *Thomas W. Morgan.* An invitation to join the line was extended to Captain Robert Carter in 1868.

CAPTAIN	CAPTAIN	CHIEF STEVEDORE
THOMAS EDGAR	JAMES W. EDGAR	HOWARD EDGAR

THREE GENERATIONS IN THE OLD BAY LINE

The operation of the "mosquito fleet" in the period which followed the war greatly enlarged the number of captains in the Bay Line's employ. The following men commanded the freighters and in many instances, they were later transferred to passenger ships on the regular run. Captain W. C. Whittle took over the *Transit* in 1869 and later served successively on the *Adelaide* and *Carolina* in 1877, then the *Virginia*[I] when she came out in 1879, and finally, as commander of the fleet, the *Georgia*[II] when she joined the Bay Line in 1887. Captain L. B. Eddens also commanded the *Adelaide*.

Two Captains Travers, Thomas and Robert, were in charge of the *Westover, Shirley,* and *State of Maryland*[I]. Captain William Porter commanded the *Louisiana* and later the *Westover* in 1873, and it will be recalled that as a result of his experience in piloting the James River that he was given the *Virginia*[I] when she transferred to the competing route on the James River in 1896. A Captain Dawes had both the *Transit* and *Petersburg* in 1877; Captain Skinner the *Westover;* and Captain Geoghegan, formerly of the propeller *Empire* on the York River, the *Roanoke* during the same year.

The little freighter *Gaston,* launched in 1881, had a goodly number of captains during her long career with the Bay Line: Jacob

—Courtesy of U. S. National Museum.

CAPT. MOSES ROGERS
Master of the first Baltimore-Norfolk
steamboat, the *Eagle* in 1815.

—From the Baltimore Sun, 1908.

CAPT. WILLIAM ROLLINS
Master of the Maryland & Virginia Steam
Boat Company ships.

—Courtesy of Mrs. W. W. Morgan.

CAPT. L. B. EDDENS
Master of the *Adelaide* in the 1870's.

—Courtesy of Old Bay Line.

CAPT. W. R. MAYO
Master of the *Louisiana* in 1874.

—Courtesy of Mrs. Franklin James.

CHIEF ENGINEER T. J. BROWNLEY
Superintended the building of the *Carolina* and *Virginia*, 1877-1879.

—Courtesy of Capt. R. S. Foster.

CAPT. W. J. BOHANNON
Master of the *Alabama* in 1898.

—Courtesy of Mrs. W. G. Lane.

CAPT. W. G. LANE
Master of the *Georgia* and *Virginia* [II].

CAPT. W. C. ALMY
First captain of the *President Warfield* in 1928.

Bloodworth, John Mason, Frank Kirby, Jim Foukes, Joseph H. Hall, and James W. Edgar, the latter being still hale and hearty, though retired ten years ago, after 51 years of service with the Line. Captain Edgar joined in 1878 and was a son of Captain Thomas Edgar, master of the *Thomas W. Morgan* in War of Secession days. His son, Howard Edgar, third generation in the Old Bay Line has already 36 years' service to his credit and is chief stevedore of the Line at Baltimore.

A very well liked shipmaster who joined the Old Bay Line in 1874 was Wyndham R. Mayo who married Admiral Decatur's daughter. Captain Mayo was a student at the U. S. Naval Academy when the war started and on his resignation in 1862 he was commissioned by the Confederate Navy serving on the C. S. S. *Patrick Henry*. After the war he continued to follow the sea and had commanded Potomac River steamers prior to joining the Bay Line. He was master of the *Louisiana* on her ill-fated voyage and was highly commended for his seamanship during the disaster.

Still another popular captain recruited from Bay Line cargo boats was R. H. Smullen. He served on the *Gaston,* and later was taken off as first mate of the *Alabama* to command the new *Raleigh* [II] in 1906. He served as master of both the *Florida*[II] and *Alabama*[II] prior to the late war, when the command of the *Raleigh* fell on Captain Joseph H. Hall likewise formerly of the *Gaston*.

Captain Wycliffe J. Bohannon, hailing from Mathews County, Virginia, a veritable breeding ground of splendid seamen, was another much beloved Old Bay Line shipmaster. Captain Bohannon served on both the *Virginia*[I] and *Carolina* and later commanded the *Georgia*[II] and *Alabama* [II]. Many people in the present employ of the company remember Captain Bohannon well. He was a splendid figure, gentle but firm, and had decided inclinations to the ministry, in fact many who knew him have said that he would have made as good a preacher as a skipper. His kinsman, Columbus Bohannon was also with the Bay Line as mate on the *Alabama*.

Captain Walter G. Lane commanded the *Georgia* in 1904 and a few years later was given the new *Virginia,* of which he was master until her sad end in 1919, two years before he retired from the sea.

Coming down to modern times, one of the most celebrated Chesapeake Bay mariners was the late William C. Almy. Captain Almy gained his initial seagoing experience as an officer on the Cape Charles-Norfolk steamers in 1884. A few years later he joined the Bay Line as master of the *Carolina* and for 44 years thereafter he commanded successively all the boats which were added to the Line, bringing out the new *Florida* in 1907, the new *State of Maryland* in 1923, and the *President Warfield* five years later. He retired in 1932, estimating that during his active career he had covered two and a half million miles in running up and down the Chesapeake.

In this the centennial year of the Old Bay Line, its oldest active employee, Captain R. S. Foster, commands the *President Warfield* with 47 years' service behind him, virtually half of the very existence of the company. Captain Foster signed on as seaman in 1893 and has progressively risen in the ranks until today he is the much respected dean of the Bay Line fleet.

His running mate, Captain John L. Marshall, a comparative "youngster" of 25 years' service joined the Line in 1915 as quartermaster and rose through second and first mates until he attained the captaincy of the *State of Maryland* in 1932, on Captain Almy's resignation.

The Old Bay Line has been fortunate in having long and faithful servants not only in its deck department but also among the engineers, pursers, and stewards, not to mention in its administrative offices ashore. Particular mention should be made of the many fine colored people who have worked for the Line. Willie T. Harris, whose celebrated trill as he announces "dinnerrr!" has long had many unsuccessful imitators. Willie has been with the line for 39 years and followed in the footsteps of his father, John Page Harris, much beloved bartender on the *Alabama,* who himself was with the Line

CAPT. J. L. MARSHALL
Master, *State of Maryland.*

CAPT. R. S. FOSTER
Master, *President Warfield.*

for 38 years. He has developed an uncanny sixth sense which enables him to spot unerringly any newly-weds among the passengers.

Other loyal colored folk with the Line for twenty years past, or recently retired, would include George Henderson, Margaret White, Dewey Lee, E. W. Billups, Janie Wilkens, C. Bumpers, T. and J. Gant, J. Haywood, S. Jones, A. Wynn, and J. Young.

In the engineering department of early times only a few names have come down to us. Albert G. Ramsey was appointed chief on the *Alabama* in 1841 and he was also on the *Medora* on her disastrous trial trip, when Duncan Ferguson, chief engineer of the ill-fated boat, was killed. George Ayres was chief on the *Georgia*[I] when the Old Bay Line began operations. Noah Bratt and Thomas James Brownley were on the *North Carolina* and *Adelaide*. The latter had joined the Line in the days of wood-burning steamers, serving on many vessels and, as senior chief engineer, superintended the installation of machinery on the *Carolina* and *Virginia* in the late 70's. Charles Reeder, a member of the illustrious family of steam engine builders, who had constructed the first engines used on the Chesapeake, served as chief on the *Thomas Kelso* when she came out in 1866. Martin Rudolph, chief engineer of the *Virginia*[I], when she was running on the James in 1896, had then been with the Line for 35 years. Wallace Hooper, chief on the *Alabama*[II] at the turn of the century also put in long and faithful service with the Line. Other Bay Line engineers included Eric Lumberson, Harry Spainer, Jim Bitters, and the Deer brothers.

Still other former members of the engineering department would include G. W. Sadler, 1890-1938; J. A. Berger, 1894-1932; and George G. Webb, 1881-1921. Coming down to modern times, Chief George M. Johnson has been on the Bay Line since he first joined as an oiler in 1913 and Chief W. F. Saunders' record began back in 1918. Mr. W. A. Miller, present port engineer, is another example of son following father in the Old Bay Line.

In the purser's department one finds Messrs. Aspirl and Wilson, "clerks" of the *Alabama* and *Georgia* when the line began. Walter

WILLIE HARRIS
Waiter on Old Bay Line steamers
since 1889.

Ball was also clerk in 1840, becoming treasurer after Thomas Sheppard in 1848, and probably established a record for service in that he had been with the Line for sixty years (fifty as treasurer) when he resigned in 1900. Lloyd B. Parkers was on the *North Carolina* in 1859 and transferred to the *Adelaide*. Colonel William Boykin was a purser in early days before taking over the company's agency at Richmond. Later on we find Walter Doyle and Charles F. Spotswood, pursers of the side-wheel *Virginia,* followed by the *Alabama.* M. T. Thurston and D. S. Cherry served on the screw steamers *Virginia*[II] and *Florida*[II] prior to the War, and today Harry C. Baker is in his twentieth year with the company as purser on the *President Warfield.*

So much for the personnel of the ships themselves. Among the executives of the organization many names stand out. Of the presidents of the company John M. Robinson's 26-year tenure of office was the longest and he succeeded popular Moor N. Falls, who had held this post for 19 years. "Captain" John R. Sherwood, although only president for 11 years, had nevertheless put in just one year short of half a century with the Line. Captain Sherwood signed on as an assistant engineer on the little freighter *New Jersey* just after the War of Secession. Although for the most part the organization of the Line at that time was made up of those with strong Confederate sympathies, President Robinson having been a former Colonel, the fact that Captain Sherwood had been an engineer in the United States Navy did not hamper his subsequent career. He succeeded Major William C. Smith as superintendent of the Line in 1874, rising later to the posts of general manager, vice-president, and president in 1907, where he was held in high regard by his fellow employees.

Other members of the organization serving the Line after the war included Thomas Kelso, one of the original directors of the company in 1840, who died in 1878 at the ripe age of 94. Thomas H. Webb was Norfolk agent in 1866, followed by William Randall, an ex-purser, twenty years later. Mr. P. S. Gornto, the present holder of this office, has served for 21 years. John Harrison Surratt, a son of unfortunate Mary Surratt, unjustly executed for complicity in Lincoln's murder, came to the line in 1870 with his brother Isaac Surratt. The former served as freight claim agent and auditor until, on his death in 1916, he was succeeded by Mr. E. P. Hook, the present general agent, now in his twenty-seventh year with the organization.

Former officers of long service with the Line would also include: Major Poore, traffic manager; Emmet Brown who retired in 1909 as treasurer and general passenger agent after 40 years' service; his successor James E. Byrd; Wilbur W. Erdman who retired in 1918 as general purchasing agent after 50 years with the company; James D. Downes who retired in 1931 as treasurer with 32 years' service; P. Byrd Thompson, retiring in 1932 as traffic manager with 22 years in the company being succeeded by the late Charles G. Rogers; and the late traveling freight agent, Theodore Butler.

It would, of course, be manifestly impossible to list all those who

JOHN HARRISON SURRATT

Auditor of the Old Bay Line from 1870 until his death in 1916.

have been and are serving faithfully on the Old Bay Line. Added to those whose names have appeared in the preceeding pages are the following who today wear well earned though invisible service stripes for twenty years or more with the organization: General Passenger Agent R. L. Jones; Purchasing Agent G. W. Schuncke; Lookoutman W. F. Pruitt, Watchman C. S. Cannon, Chief Manifest Clerk A. H. Bettien, Receiving Clerk A. H. Bowen; Accountant L. A. Buckley; Receiving Clerk G. S. Deady; Clerk S. O. Hall, Clerk E. J. Karl, Chief Delivery Clerk C. M. King, Receiving Clerk J. A. Lupton, Assistant Chief Stevedore A. M. Lutz, Pier Ticket Agent John Moale, a direct descent of John C. Moale, general agent of the Old Bay Line in 1840.

Chief Clerk to General Agent J. A. Moeller, Watchman J. R.

Parsons, Assistant Agent H. J. Schafer, Freight and Passenger Representative G. L. Stern, Secretary to Freight Traffic Manager R. W. Sullivan, City Freight Agent D. J. Savage, City Ticket Agent J. A. Thomas, Clerk H. W. Lyons, and Chief Delivery Clerk C. D. Griffin.

Length of service in an organization is proof positive of faithful and devoted work. However, it gives an unbalanced picture in that junior members of the company are denied this overt evidence of their loyalty. One can not measure merely in terms of years that intangible quality which has long contributed materially to the success and efficiency of the Old Bay Line. There are a very great many present employees who, despite the fact that they have not yet had time to build up a service record, are nevertheless as interested and faithful workers as their seniors in the organization. It is on the shoulders of these men that the success of the Bay Line of to-morrow depends, a trust which, it is obvious, will be fostered down through many years to come. The Old Bay Line has had good ships, but this would not have been enough without the loyalty of the personnel which for a hundred years has kept the Bay Line at the forefront of American steamship lines. With justification then, the Old Bay Line, beloved by countless travelers the world over, is proud of the record it has maintained through the vicissitudes of a century and embarks on the second hundred years of operation with the certain knowledge that future generations will maintain the illustrious record of the past.

—*Courtesy of Miss M. C. Wisong.*

Appendix

THE INCORPORATORS OF THE B. S. P. CO., 1839-40

WM. McDONALD

ROBERT A. TAYLOR

JOEL VICKERS

JOHN S. McKIM

JOHN B. HOWELL

BENJAMIN BUCK

SAMUEL McDONALD

THOMAS KELSO

ANDREW F. HENDERSON

AND OTHERS

ORIGINAL DIRECTORS OF THE B. S. P. CO.

A. F. HENDERSON, President

J. S. McKIM

BENJ. BUCK

JOEL VICKERS

J. B. HOWELL

R. A. TAYLOR

THOS. KELSO

GEN'L WM. McDONALD

ORIGINAL SUBSCRIBERS

C. D. BLANEY

JOHN C. MOALE

JOSEPH TODHUNTER

HUGH W. EVANS

JOHN BROWN HOWELL

CALEB GOODWIN & CO.

LYNCH & CRAFT

PRESIDENTS OF THE B. S. P. CO.

		Years
1840-1842	ANDREW FISHER HENDERSON	2
1842-1848	ROBERT A. TAYLOR	6
1848-1867	MOOR N. FALLS	19
1867-1893	JOHN MONCURE ROBINSON	26
1893-1899	RICHARD CURZON HOFFMAN	6
1899-1904	JOHN SKELTON WILLIAMS	5
1904-1906	J. M. BARR	2
1906-1907	ALFRED WALTER	1
1907-1918	JOHN ROBERTS SHERWOOD	11
[1918-1920	Federal Control, KEY COMPTON, Director	2]
1918-1927	S. DAVIES WARFIELD	9
1927-	LEGH R. POWELL, JR.	

LIST OF PRESENT OFFICERS OF THE BALTIMORE STEAM PACKET COMPANY,

Pier 10, Light Street, Baltimore, Maryland.

L. R. POWELL, JR.,
President

L. H. WINDHOLZ,
Chairman of the Board

R. E. DUNN, *Vice-President*

R. P. JONES, *Vice-President, Finance and Accounting*

R. L. JONES, *General Passenger Agent*

E. P. HOOK, *General Agent, Baltimore*

P. S. GORNTO, *General Agent, Norfolk*

T. B. ALFRIEND, *Freight Traffic Manager*

W. A. MILLER, *Port Engineer*

G. W. SCHUNCKE, *Purchasing Agent*

LIST OF FLEET PERSONNEL FOR THE STEAMERS ON REGULAR NIGHTLY SERVICE

President Warfield:

R. S. FOSTER, Master
R. D. EMERSON, First Officer
GEO. R. CLARK, Second Officer
WM. F. SAUNDERS, Chief Engineer
C. M. WALKER, First Assistant Eng'r.
H. R. CLIFTON, Second Assistant Eng'r.
H. C. BAKER, Purser
B. T. DONOHO, Chief Steward

State of Maryland:

J. L. MARSHALL, Master
P. L. PARKER, First Officer
W. E. RILEE, Second Officer
GEO. M. JOHNSON, Chief Engineer
GEO. H. DEAGLE, First Assistant Eng'r.
D. K. WILLIAMS, Second Assist. Eng'r.
W. E. RICE, Purser
WM. BAUERS, Chief Steward

MODERN SCHEDULE OF OLD BAY LINE STEAMERS ON TYPICAL SOUTHBOUND VOYAGE

Northbound voyages leave Norfolk and arrive Baltimore at the same hours. 12 hours elapsed time.

Landmark.	Distance between	Statute miles from Baltimore	Time between	Schedule
Leave BALTIMORE	0.0	0.0	0:00	6:30 P. M.
Pass LAZARETTO	3.0	3.0	:25	6:55 P. M.
Pass FORT CARROLL	4.0	7.0	:20	7:15 P. M.
Pass SEVEN FOOT KNOLL	7.5	14.5	:25	7:40 P. M.
Pass SANDY POINT	9.9	24.4	:37	8:17 P. M.
Pass THOMAS' POINT	8.6	33.0	:30	8:47 P. M.
Pass SHARP'S ISLAND	18.1	51.1	1:00	9:47 P. M.
Pass COVE POINT	17.6	68.7	1:01	10:48 P. M.
Pass SMITH'S POINT	36.6	105.3	2:14	1:02 A. M.
Pass WINDMILL POINT	19.4	124.7	1:08	2:10 A. M.
Pass WOLF TRAP	14.3	139.0	:49	2:59 A. M.
Pass YORK SPIT	12.7	151.7	:44	3:43 A. M.
Pass BACK RIVER	8.1	159.8	:32	4:15 A. M.
Pass THIMBLE LIGHT	8.2	168.0	:30	4:45 A. M.
Arrive OLD POINT COMFORT	4.0	172.0	:15	5:00 A. M.
Leave OLD POINT COMFORT	0.0	172.0	:30	5:30 A. M.
Arrive NORFOLK	13.3	185.3	1:00	6:30 A. M.

SCHEDULE SOUTHBOUND IN 1819

J. B. Marestier made the trip from Baltimore to Norfolk on the *Virginia* in the year 1819. The following table has been made up from times and distances given in his *Mémoire sur les Bateaux à Vapeur des États-Unis* (1824). Nautical miles given by Marestier have been converted to statute miles. The modern run is 185.3 miles as oposed to 180.1 miles in 1819 with shallow draft steamboats.

Landmark.	Distance between	Statute miles from Baltimore	Time between	Total time
Left dock BALTIMORE	0.0	0.0	:00	not given
Passed FELLS POINT	.7	.7	:05	:05
Passed NORTH POINT (Patapsco Entrance)	10.6	11.3	1:17	1:22
Passed SOUTH POINT (Bodkin Point)	4.3	15.6	:33	1:55
Passed OLD POINT LIGHT	153.0	168.6	17:35	19:30
Arrived NORFOLK LIGHT	11.5	180.1	1:40	21:10

THE FLEET OF STEAMERS OWNED AND OPERATED BY THE OLD BAY LINE FROM 1840 TO DATE. Compiled from Company records, Baltimore Customs House Records, Lists of Merchant Vessels of the U. S., and other sources. Arranged in order of acquisition by the Line. Due to changes in the methods of computation neither tonnage nor horse-power figures are comparable between early and modern vessels.

Pocahontas: Wood, side-wheel, passenger; 428 tons; 138.0' l. x 30.0' b. x 11.0' d. Built at Baltimore, Md., in 1829 by Beacham & Gardiner for James River Service of the Maryland and Virginia Steam Boat Company. Vertical beam engine by Charles Reeder, 50" diam. x 78" stroke, 100 H.P. Acquired by B.S. P.Co. in **1840** for $8,000. Sold in 1845 to the Powhatan Steam Boat Company. The original dimensions of the *Pocahontas* were 116.6' x 35.5' x 11.1'.

South Carolina: Wood, side-wheel, passenger; 466 tons; 172.0' l. x 23.0' b. x 12.5' d. Built at Baltimore, Md., in 1835 by John Robb for Norfolk-Charleston service of the Atlantic Line. Cross-head engine by Watchman & Bratt, 44" diam. x 102" stroke, 140 H.P. Acquired by B.S.P.Co. in **1840** for $15,000. In 1842 the owners resolved either to sell or dismantle the *South Carolina.*

Georgia [I]: Wood, side-wheel, passenger; 551 tons; 194.0' l. x 24.0' b. x 12.2' d. Built at Baltimore, Md., in 1836 by John Robb for Norfolk-Charleston service of the Atlantic Line. Lever-beam engine by Charles Reeder, 46" diam. x 114" stroke, 140 H.P. Acquired by B.S.P.Co. in **1840** for $32,000. Reported "much damaged" in 1856. Chartered by U. S. War Department, 1863. Sold by B.S.P.Co. in 1865 to James A. Hooper.

Jewess: Wood, side-wheel, passenger; 352 tons; 173.5' l. x 22.8' b. x 9.1' d. Built at Baltimore, Md., in 1838 by W. & G. Gardiner for Maryland & Virginia Steam Boat Company. Lever beam engine by Wells, Miller & Clark, 40" diam. x 132" stroke, 160 H.P. Acquired by B.S.P.Co. in **1840** for $15,250. Burned at dock Jan. 11, 1848. Rebuilt and lengthened by Flannegan & Trimble. Public sale at auction advertised by B.S.P.Co. for July 1, 1852. Dimensions given 200.0' x 24.0' x 9.2'. Reported stranded or foundered in 1856.

Alabama [I]: Wood, side-wheel, passenger; 676 tons; 210.0' l. x 24.7' b. x 13.5' d. Built at Baltimore, Md., in 1838 by Levin H. Dunkin for Maryland & Virginia Steam Boat Co. Vertical beam engine by Charles Reeder & Sons, 48" diam. x 126" stroke, 200 H.P. Acquired (?) by B.S.P.Co. in **1841**. Cost not given. Sold by them to the Havana & New Orleans Steam Boat Company in 1841 and left for New Orleans Oct. 6, 1841. Reported lost or stranded in 1852.

Norwich: Wood, side-wheel, passenger; said to have been on temporary charter to B.S.P.Co. in **1841**.

Medora: Wood, side-wheel, passenger; Tonnage not given; 180.0' l. x 23.6' x 9.6' d. Built at Baltimore, Md., in 1842 by Brown & Collyer for B.S.P.Co. Lever-beam engine by John Watchman, 42" diam. x 126" stroke. The *Medora* exploded on her trial trip on April 15, **1842**. Rebuilt as *Herald.*

Herald: (#11936) (Ex-*Medora*): Wood, side-wheel, passenger; 329 tons; 184.0′ l. x 24.0′ b. x 9.6′ d. Built at Baltimore, Md., in 1842 by Brown & Collyer for B.S.P.Co. Vertical beam engine by John Watchman, 42″ diam. x 126″ stroke, 250 H.P. Acquired by B.S.P.Co. in **1842**, price not given. Rebuilt and lengthened in 1849 to 215.0′ x 25.0′ x 10.0′. In 1867 the *Herald* transferred her registry to the Hudson River. Dropped from the Register as "abandoned" in 1885.

Alice: Wood, side-wheel, passenger; 326 tons; 167.6′ l. x 23.4′ b. x 8.8′ d. Built at Brooklyn, N. Y., in 1845 by Divine Burtis. Lever beam engine, 40″ diam. x 132″. Acquired by B.S.P.Co. a 11/32 interest for $12,093 in **1845**, port of registry is Richmond, Va. Interest sold by B.S.P.Co. in 1848. At New London, Conn., in 1850. Burned on July 22, 1852, at Bridgeport, Conn. The *Alice* was used by the B.S.P.Co. on James River service.

Mount Vernon: Iron, side-wheel, passenger; 195.0′ long. Built at Philadelphia, Pa., in 1846 by Birely for Washington & Fredericksburg Steam Boat Co. Vertical beam engine. Acquired by B.S.P.Co. in **1847** for $2,650 and used on Appomattox River service. Sold by B.S.P.Co. in 1852 (?).

North Carolina: Wood, side-wheel, passenger; 1,120 gross, 861 net tons; 239.3′ l. x 35.5′ b. x 11.2′ d. Built at Baltimore, Md., in 1852 by Cooper & Butler for B.S.P.Co. Vertical beam engine by Murray and Hazelhurst, 60″ diam. x 132″ stroke. Acquired by B.S.P.Co. in **1852** for $111,272. Burned at sea on route Norfolk, Jan. 29, 1859. Unsuccessful attempts made to salvage her machinery.

Louisiana: (#14539) Wood, side-wheel, passenger; 1,126 gross tons, 266.2′ l. x 36.0′ b. x 12.2′ d. Built at Baltimore, Md., in 1854 by Cooper & Butler for B.S.P.Co. Vertical beam engine by Charles Reeder, 60″ diam. x 132″ stroke, 2,037 H.P. Acquired by B.S.P.Co. in **1854** for $234,197. Rebuilt by William Skinner & Son, Baltimore, in 1871. Rammed and sunk Nov. 14, 1874, by *Falcon.* Hull total loss, machinery salvaged and later used in *Carolina,* 1877.

Adelaide: (#85) Wood, side-wheel, passenger; 972 gross, 734 net tons; 233.0′ l. x 32.1′ b. x 8.8′ d. Built at Greenpoint, L. I., N. Y., in 1854 by Lupton and McDermott for Calais Steamboat Co., Boston-St. John, N. B., service. Vertical beam engine by Guion Boardman & Co., 50″ diam. x 144″ stroke, 1,370 H.P. Acquired to replace *North Carolina* by B.S.P.Co. in **1859** for $91,258. Temporary charter to U. S. Navy in 1861. Sold by B.S.P.Co. in 1879 to Harlan and Hollingsworth, Wilmington, Del. As Long Branch, N. J., steamer was rammed and sunk June 19, 1880, by *Grand Republic* in New York harbor.

Georgeanna: (#10043) Iron, side-wheel, passenger; 738 gross, 501 net tons; 199.1′ l. x 30.0′ b. x 9.6′ d. Built at Wilmington, Del., in 1859 by Harland and Hollingsworth for G. R. H. Leffler. Vertical beam engine from *Gladiator,* 44″ diam. x 132″ stroke, 1,119 H.P. Acquired by B.S.P.Co. in **1860** for $58,175.

April 12, 1864, collision with U. S. S. *Iroquois*. Sold by B.S.P.Co. to Potomac Steamboat Co. in 1869. Transferred registry to New York in 1888; renamed *Colonia* in 1901; broken up in 1902.

Philadelphia: (#12474) Wood, side-wheel, passenger; 504 tons; 201.0′ l. x 29.0′ b. x 9.0′ d. Built at Philadelphia, Pa., in 1860 by Reanie, Neafie & Co. for Seaboard & Roanoke Railroad. Vertical Beam engine by Reanie, Neafie & Co., 45″ diam. x 132″ stroke, 384 H.P. Acquired B.S.P.Co. in **1860** for $93,000. Sold by B.S.P.Co. in 1861 (?) to Potomac Steamboat Co. Renamed *Ironsides*. Lost on Hog Island Shoals, Aug. 29, 1873.

William Selden: Wood, side-wheel, passenger; 378 tons, 18.0′ l. x 24.8′ b. 8.6′ d. Built at Washington, D. C., in 1851 by George Page for account of builder. Vertical beam engine. Acquired by B.S.P.Co. in **1860** for $17,465. Expressly burned at dock May 10, 1862, during evacuation of Norfolk by Confederates.

Thomas A. Morgan: (#24038) Iron, side-wheel, passenger; 681 gross, 520 net tons; 189.3′ l. x 28.4′ b. x 8.9′ d. Built at Wilmington, Del., in 1854 by Harlan & Hollingsworth for Rockhill, Burdon, and Cone. Vertical beam engine by Harlan & Hollingsworth, 44″ diam. x 120″ stroke, 800 H.P. Acquired by B.S.P.Co. in **1862** for $56,695. 1862, official U. S. War Department mail steamer. 1867, traded for *New Jersey* by B.S.P.Co. Dropped from Register in 1879. (Register confuses two vessels both named *Thomas A. Morgan,* #24038 and #24748).

Eolus: (#7184) Wood, side-wheel, passenger; 731 gross, 275 net tons; 144.0′ l. x 25.0′ b. x 10.2′ d. Built at Newburgh, N. Y., in 1864 by Thomas Marvel. Vertical beam engine by Washington Iron Works, 40″ diam. x 96″ stroke, 285 H.P. Acquired by B.S.P.Co. in **1865** for $11,314. Used by them on local routes out of Norfolk. 1869, sold to Newport, R. I., and used on Narragansett Bay. Dismantled in 1894.

Thomas Kelso: (#24039) Iron, side-wheel, passenger; 1,430 tons; 236.9′ l. x 35.4′ b. x 10.4′ d. Built at Chester, Pa., in 1865 by Reaney, Son & Co., for B.S.P.Co. Vertical beam engine by Reaney, Son & Co., 53″ diam. x 132″ stroke, 800 H.P. Acquired by B.S.P.Co. in **1865** for $204,020. December 8, 1866, explodes steam drum off Wolf Trap, towed to Portsmouth for repairs. Sold by B.S.P.Co. in 1869 to Marshall O. Roberts, New York. 1872, home port Providence, R. I. Reported lost at sea Mar. 31, 1884.

George Leary: (#10045) Wood, side-wheel, passenger; 810 gross, 621 net tons; 237.0′ l. x 33.0′ b. x 10.0′ d. Built at Brooklyn, N. Y., in 1864 by Thomas Stack for Leary Bros. Vertical beam engine by James Murphy & Co., 50″ diam. x 144″ stroke, 1,872 H.P. Was on opposition line to B.S.P.Co. Acquired by B.S.P.Co. in **1867** for $235,125. Sold by B.S.P.Co. in 1879 to M. Robinson, Georgetown, D. C., for Potomac River service. Dropped from Register as "lost" Dec. 30, 1901.

New Jersey: Wood, screw, freighter; 305 tons; 166.5′ l. x 22.6′ b. x 9.0′ d. Built at Baltimore, Md., in 1862. Simple cylinder reciprocating engine. Acquired by B.S.P.Co. in **1867** in trade for *Thomas A. Morgan* and $2,000. Total loss by fire at sea Feb. 26, 1870.

Transit: (#24368) Wood, screw, freighter; 478 gross, 408 net tons; 149.0′ x. 25.0′ b. x 9.4′ d. Built at Brooklyn, N. Y., in 1864 for Montauk Steam Navigation Co. Simple cylinder reciprocating engine, 32″ diam. x 26″ stroke, 500 H.P. Acquired by B.S.P.Co. in **1869** for $32,694. Used on Canton Inside Freight Line. Sold in 1883 to New York. Renamed *John Lenox* in 1883; renamed *Reserve* in 1914; abandoned at Catskill, N. Y., in 1938.

Roanoke: (#21986) Iron, screw, freighter; 531 gross, 431 net tons; 168.7′ l. x 27.0′ b. 9.3′ d. Built at Wilmington, Del., in 1871 by Harlan & Hollingsworth for B.S.P.Co. Simple cylinder reciprocating engine by Harlan & Hollingsworth, 34″ diam. x 34″ stroke, 713 H.P. Acquired by B.S.P.Co. in **1871** for $64,544. Used on Canton Inside Freight Line. Sold in 1887 to I. H. Panly, Milwaukee, Wis. Dropped from Register 1906 at Tampa, Fla.

Westover: (#80390) Iron, screw, freighter; 577 gross, 416 net tons; 163.0′ l. x 28.0′ b. x 12.4′ d. Built at Wilmington, Del., in 1873 by Harlan & Hollingsworth for B.S.P.Co. Simple cylinder reciprocating engine by Harlan & Hollingsworth, 34″ diam. x 34″ stroke, 492 H.P. Acquired by B.S.P.Co. in **1873** for $73,214. Used on James River Freight Line. Sold in 1887 to I. H. Panly, Milwaukee, Wis. 1897, home port Chicago. 1901, home port Philadelphia. 1906, renamed *Dover.* Stranded in St. Johns River, Oct. 2, 1912.

Vesta: (#25863) Iron, side-wheel, tug (?); 219 gross, 147 net tons; 102.0′ l. x 18.8′ b. x 4.4′ d. Built at Norfolk, Va., in 1870 for Seaboard and Roanoke Railroad. Vertical beam engine, 29 H.P. Acquired by B.S.P.Co. in **1874** for $5,170. One half interest sold in 1875 by B.S.P.Co. to Wilmington, Weldon & Seaboard Railroad. Registered at Washington, N. C. Dropped from Register in 1889.

Shirley: (#115265) Iron, screw, freighter; 576 gross tons; 165.0′ l. x 28.0′ b. x 12.0′ d. Built at Wilmington, Del., in 1874 by Harlan & Hollingsworth for B. S. P. Co. Simple cylinder reciprocating engine by Harlan & Hollingsworth, 34″ diam. x 34″ stroke, 491 H.P. Acquired by B.S.P.Co. in **1874** for $70,538. Used on James River Freight Line. Sold by B.S.P.Co. in 1877 to Baltimore, Chesapeake & Richmond Steam Boat Co. of Baltimore for York River service. Burned, Nov. 28, 1880, and rebuilt as *West Point.* Burned again Dec. 26, 1881.

Seaboard: (#115348) Iron, screw, freighter; 662 gross, 563 net tons; 184.5′ l. x 28.7′ b. x 12.3′ d. Built at Wilmington, Del., in 1874 by Harlan & Hollingsworth for B.S.P.Co. Simple cylinder reciprocating engine by Harlan & Hollingsworth, 34″ diam. x 42″ stroke, 693 H.P. Acquired by B.S.P.Co. in **1874** for $78,852. Used on Canton Inside Freight Line. Sold by B.S.P.Co. in 1898 to

Hartford & New York Transportation Co. of New York. Used as freighter New York to Bridgeport, Conn. Laid-up in 1931-1933. In 1934 hull rebuilt as coastwise tanker by L. D. Pierce. Owned by North Atlantic Trading Co., Providence, R. I. 450 H.P. Worthington Diesel engine installed. In operation today.

Petersburg: (#19542) (ex-*Western World*) Wood, screw, freighter; 675 tons; 178.8′ 1. x 34.3′ b. x 8.1′ d. Built at Brooklyn, N. Y., in 1856 by William Collyer for Sherman & Mull. Purchased by U. S. Navy as *Western World* Sept. 21, 1861. Purchased by H. R. Hazelhurst, June 24, 1865. Purchased by Powhatan Steamboat Co. on Nov. 21, 1865, and renamed *Petersburg.* Purchased by B.S.P.Co. in **1874** for $40.000. Used on Canton Inside Freight Line. Sold by B.S.P.Co. in 1879 to Boston, Mass. Converted to barge in 1880. Tonnage reduced to 497 gross. Reported "lost" Feb. 7, 1895.

State of Virginia[I]: (#22096) (ex-*Northerner*) Wood, side-wheel, passenger; 1,061 tons; 238.2′ 1. x 31.1′ b. x 12.5′ d. Built at Ogdenburg, N. Y., in 1849 for Lake Erie service. Vertical beam engine, 60″ diam. x 132″ stroke, 600 H.P. 1865, purchased by Powhatan Steamboat Co. from U. S. Government after Civil War. Purchased by B.S.P.Co. in **1875** for $13,964. Broken-up, 1875 and machinery used in *Florida,* 1876.

State of Maryland[I]: (#22095) (ex-*Atlantic*) Wood, side-wheel, passenger; 774 tons; 186.9′ 1. x 33.0′ b. x 11.6′ d. Built at Brooklyn, N. Y., in 1857 by Devine Burtis as East River, New York, ferry boat. Vertical beam engine, 45″ diam. x 132″ stroke, 662 H.P. Purchased in 1863 by U. S. Navy, renamed *Commodore Read,* dimensions and tonnage altered. Purchased by Powhatan Steamboat Co. in 1865 and renamed *State of Maryland.* Acquired by B.S.P.Co. in **1875** for $7,506. Wrecked Mar. 31, 1876.

Ellie Knight: (#7062) Wood, screw, freighter; 298 gross, 207 net tons, 155.0′ 1. x 23.0′ b. x 7.8′ d. Built at Philadelphia, Pa., in 1863 by Birely, Hilman & Co. for New York-Philadelphia Outside Line. Simple cylinder reciprocating engine, 32″ diam. x 30″ stroke, 372 H.P. In 1865 on Peoples Line, Baltimore to Richmond. Acquired by B.S.P.Co. in **1875** for $5,755. Sold by B.S.P.Co. in 1876 to Steamboat Company of Boston for Boston-Gloucester, Mass., service. 1884, home port New Orleans. Dropped from Register in 1887.

Cockade City: (#9050) (ex-*Burnside* (?) or ex-*Reno* (?), later ex-*Fannie Lehr)* Wood, side-wheel, freighter; 306 tons; 154.9′ 1. x 21.6′ b. x 5.3′ d. Built at Baltimore, Md., in 1863 by Norman Wiard for U. S. Government as transport. 1865, sold to Robert Lehr and renamed *Fannie Lehr.* 1874, rebuilt at Baltimore and renamed *Cockade City.* Purchased by B.S.P.Co. in **1875** for $10,000. Sold by B.S.P.Co. in 1877 to Frank Debelius, Potomac River Barge Co., Baltimore, Md. Converted to unrigged barge, 168 tons, in 1877. Dropped from Register 1884.

Florida[I]: (#120257) Wood, side-wheel, passenger; 1,279 gross, 900 net tons; 259.0′ l. x 36.1′ b. x 13.6′ d. Built at Baltimore, Md., in 1876 by Wm. Skinner & Son for B.S.P.Co. Vertical beam engine from *State of Virginia*[I] (ex-*Northerner*), installed by James Clark & Co., 60″ diam. x 132″ stroke, 2,513 H.P. Acquired by B.S.P.Co. in 1876 for $231,207. Sold by B.S.P.Co. to James H. Gregory, N. Y., for scrap. Sunk April 28, 1892, while being towed to New York.

Raleigh[I]: (#110136) Wood, screw, freighter; 593 gross, 391 net tons; 169.0′ l. x 30.2′ b. x 16.0′ d. Built at Baltimore, Md., in 1873 by J. S. Beacham & Bro. Oscillating (?) engine, 399 H.P. Acquired by B.S.P.Co. in 1877 for $12,916. Sold by B.S.P.Co. in 1877 to Baltimore. Later owned by Atlantic & Gulf Steam Transportation Co. Dropped from Register, 1897.

Carolina: (#125595) Iron, side-wheel, passanger; 984 gross, 831 net tons; 251.0′ l. x 34.7′ b. x 7.9′ d. Built at Wilmington, Del., in 1877 by Harlan & Hollingsworth for B.S.P.Co. Vertical beam engine from *Louisiana* (Charles Reeder), 60″ diam. x 132″ stroke, 800 H.P. Acquired by B.S.P.Co. in 1877 for $198,963. Sold by B.S.P.Co. in 1893 to Richlieu & Ontario Navigation Co., Toronto, Canada, for St. Lawrence River service. Renamed *Murray Bay* in 1907; renamed *Cape Diamond* in 1921; dropped from Lloyd's in 1933.

Virginia[I]: (#25955) Iron, side-wheel, passenger; 990 gross, 665 net tons; 251.0′ l. x 34.7′ b. x 7.9′ d. Built at Wilmington, Del., in 1879 by Harlan & Hollingsworth for B.S.P.Co. Vertical beam engine by Harlan & Hollingsworth, 50″ diam. x 132″ stroke, 800 H.P. Acquired by B.S.P.Co. in 1879 for $211,479. In 1896 used by B.S.P.Co. on new James River Line. Sold by B.S.P.Co. in 1900 to Joseph R. Wainwright. 1902 ran under charter on Joy Line. 1903 sold to the Richlieu & Ontario Navigation Co., Toronto, Canada, for St. Lawrence River service. Renamed *Tadousac* in 1905. Dropped from Lloyd's in 1927.

Gaston: (#85685) Iron, screw, freighter; 847 gross, 464 net tons; 212.0′ l. x 35.5′ b. x 19.0′ d. Built at Wilmington, Del., in 1881 by Harlan & Hollingsworth for B.S.P.Co. Compound reciprocating engine by Harlan & Hollingsworth, 26″ and 44″ diam. x 36″ stroke, 540 H.P. Acquired by B.S.P.Co. in 1881 for $119,545. Sold by B.S.P.Co. in 1920 to Gulfport (Miss.) Fruit and S. S. Co. Dropped from Register in 1935.

Georgia[II]: (#85961) Iron, screw, passanger; 1,749 gross, 1,188 net tons; 280.1′ l. x 40.0′ b. x 15.0′ d. Built at Wilmington, Del., in 1887 by Harlan & Hollingsworth for B.S.P.Co. Compound reciprocating engine by Harlan & Hollingsworth, 34″ and 64″ diam. x 42″ stroke, 1,950 H.P. Acquired by B.S.P.Co. in 1887 for $252,263. Sold by B.S.P.Co. in 1909 to Hartford & New York Transportation Co. Operated on Providence Line. Became floating night club at New Haven in 1930. Scrapped at Baltimore in 1937.

Alabama[II]: (#106995) Steel, screw, passenger; 1,938 gross, 1,378 net tons; 293.8' l. x 54.0' b. x 16.0' d. Built at Sparrows Point, Md., in 1893 by Maryland Steel Co. for B.S.P.Co. Four cylinder triple-expansion reciprocating engine by Maryland Steel Co., 24½", 40", & (2) 47" diam. x 42" stroke, 3,400 H.P. Acquired by B.S.P.Co. in 1893 for $291,993. Sold by B.S.P.Co. in 1928 to Progress Improvement Co., Seattle, Wash. Converted to oil-burning auto ferry in 1928 and renamed *City of Victoria*. In 1939 sold to Puget Sound Bridge & Dredging Co. for floating hotel at Sitka, Alaska.

Elsie: (#136368) Steel, screw, tug; 39 gross, 19 net tons; 57.6' l. x 14.8' b. x 7.2' d. Built at Baltimore, Md., in 1893 by R. M. Spedden for B.S.P.Co. Compound reciprocating engine, 9" and 16" diam. x 18" stroke, 100 H.P. Acquired by B.S.P.Co. in 1893. Exchanged by B.S.P.Co. in 1923 for tug *Mary O'Riorden* plus $5,000, to Norfolk Lighterage Co. 1939, laid-up by Wood Towing Co., Norfolk.

Enoch Pratt: Iron, side-wheel, passenger. On temporary charter to B.S.P.Co. in 1896.

Tred-Avon: Wood, screw, passenger. On temporary charter to B.S.P.Co. in 1896.

Tennessee: (#145783) Steel, twin-screw, passenger; 1,240 gross, 743 net tons; 245.0' l. x 38.5' b. x 15.8' d. Built at Wilmington, Del., in 1898 by Harlan & Hollingsworth for B.S.P.Co. Two triple-expansion reciprocating engines by Harlan & Hollingsworth, each 18", 28", & 45" diam. x 30" stroke, 3,200 H.P. Acquired by B.S.P.Co. in 1898 for $158,691. Sold by B.S.P.Co. in 1906 to Joy Steamship Co., N. Y. Used on Long Island Sound until 1930. Renamed *Romance* in 1935 and used by Charles L. Ellis as an excursion steamer. Sunk in Boston Harbor on Sept. 9, 1936, collision with *New York*.

City of Philadelphia: Wood, screw, freighter. On temporary charter to B.S.P.Co. in 1904.

Virginia[II]: (#202467) Steel, screw, passenger; 2,027 gross, 1,378 net tons; 296.' l. x 44.1' b. x 15.7' d. Built at Wilmington, Del., in 1905 by Harlan & Hollingsworth for B.S.P.Co. Four cylinder triple-expansion reciprocating engine by Harlan & Hollingsworth, 24½", 40", & (2) 47" diam. x 42" stroke, 2,850 H.P. Acquired by B.S.P.Co. in 1905 for $318,318. After gallery added 1909. Burned at sea May 24, 1919, on route Norfolk, total loss.

Raleigh[II]: (#203422) Steel, screw, freighter; 1,185 gross, 805 net tons; 222.5' l. x 33.0' b. x 21.3' d. Built at Sparrows Point, Md., in 1906 by Maryland Steel Co. for B.S.P.Co. Three cylinder triple-expansion reciprocating engine by Maryland Steel Co., 19", 31", & 56" diam. x 30" stroke, 1,200 H.P. Acquired by B.S.P.Co. in 1906 for $132,914. Sold by B.S.P.Co. in 1924 to Saginaw & Bay City S. S. Co., Port Huron, Mich. Acquired by Colonial Navigation Co., N. Y., in 1929 and renamed *Marion*. In operation today under Philippine ownership.

Florida[II]: (#204629) Steel, screw, passenger; 2,185 gross, 1,486 net tons; 298.0′ l. x 45.0′ b. x 16.1′ d. Built at Sparrows Point, Md., in 1907 by Maryland Steel Co. for B.S.P.Co. Four cylinder triple-expansion reciprocating engine by Maryland Steel Co., 24½″, 40″, & (2) 47″ diam. x 42″ stroke, 2,600 H.P. Acquired by B.S.P.Co. in **1907** for $364,782. Sold by B.S.P.Co. in 1924 to Monticello S. S. Co., San Francisco, Cal. Converted to auto ferry 1924 and renamed *Calistoga*. Taken over in 1935 by S. P. G. G. Ferries. Withdrawn from service in 1937. Now being held for sale.

Benjamin B. Odell: (#208448) Steel, screw, passenger. Chartered by B.S.P.Co. from Central Hudson Steamboat Co. **1920-1921** during re-boilering of *Alabama*.

State of Maryland[II]: (#222636) Steel, screw, passenger; 1,783 gross, 669 net tons; 320.0′ l. x 56.6′ b. x 16.9′ d. Built at Wilmington, Del., in 1922 by Pusey & Jones Corp. for B.S.P.Co. Four cylinder triple-expansion reciprocating engine by Pusey & Jones Corp., 24½″, 40″, & (2) 47″ diam. x 42″ stroke, 2,800 H.P. Acquired by B.S.P.Co. in **1923** for $718,778. Converted to oil-burning 1933. In operation today on Old Bay Line.

State of Virginia[II]: (#222715) Steel, screw, passenger; 1,783 gross, 674 net tons; 320.0′ l. x 56.6′ b. x 16.9′ d. Built at Wilmington, Del., in 1923 by Pusey & Jones Corp. for B.S.P.Co. Four cylinder triple-expansion reciprocating engine by Pusey & Jones Corp., 24½″, 40″, & (2) 47″ diam. x 42″ stroke, 2,800 H.P. Acquired by B.S.P.Co. in **1923** for $717,105. Converted to oil-burning in 1939. In operation today as extra boat of Old Bay Line.

Mary O'Riorden: (#10664) (Ex-*Glen Iris*) Iron, screw, tug; 64 gross, 34 net tons; 78.7′ l. x 16.5′ b. x 81′ d. Built at Buffalo, N. Y., in 1863 by David Bell. Simple cylinder reciprocating engine, 24″ diam. x 22″ stroke, 200 H.P. Renamed *Mary O'Riorden* in 1909. Acquired by B.S.P.Co. in **1923** from Norfolk Lighterage Co. in exchange for tug *Elsie* and $3,000. Sold by B.S.P.Co. in 1927 to C. A. Jording, Baltimore, Md. Converted to diesel, 350 H.P., in 1932. 1939, owned by Capt. T. Nilsson and used on N. Y. State Barge Canal. Now in operation.

President Warfield: (#227753) Steel, screw, passenger; 1,814 gross, 706 net tons; 320.0′ l. x 56.6′ b. x 16.9′ d. Built at Wilmington, Del., in 1928 by Pusey & Jones Corp. for B.S.P.Co. Four cylinder triple-expansion reciprocating engine by Pusey & Jones Corp., 24½″, 40″, & (2) 47″ diam. x 42″ stroke, 2,800 H.P. Acquired by B.S.P.Co. in **1928** for $959,970. Converted to oil-burning in 1933. In operation today as flagship of Old Bay Line.

Alcyone: (#204069) Steel, screw, freighter; 440 gross, 229 net tons; 155.6′ l. x 30.0′ b. x 17.6′ d. Built at South Boston, Mass. in 1907 by George Lawley & Son Corp. for H. W. Putnam, Jr., as private yacht. Steam plant replaced in 1922 by diesel-electric drive by Winton Eng. Corp., 12 cylinders, 11″ diam. x 14″

stroke, 450 H.P. Converted from yacht to merchant service 1935. Acquired by B.S.P.Co. in **1936**, for $3,600 plus repairs and alterations. Now held by Old Bay Line as extra freight boat.

Marguerite: (#14G160) Wood, screw, launch; 26.6′ l. x 9.9′ b. x 2.0′ d. Built at West Norfolk, Va., in 1936 by W. F. Dunn Marine Railway for B.S.P.Co. Gasoline engine, Chrysler, 53 H.P. Acquired by B.S.P.Co., May **1936** for $1,500. Used by Old Bay Line as ship-to-ship tender at Ocean View on summer house boat cruises.

Bibliography

Manuscript Sources.

BALTIMORE CUSTOMS HOUSE.—Enrollment Books.

BALTIMORE STEAM PACKET COMPANY.—Extracts of Minutes of the Board of Directors, 1840-1940.—Contracts entered into by the Company.—Agreement of January 11, 1877, between B.S.P.Co. and Baltimore, Chesapeake, and Richmond Steamboat Company.—Miscellaneous company correspondence.

MARINERS' MUSEUM. 4 Portfolios of plans of vessels, hull and machinery, constructed by the Harlan & Hollingsworth Co., Wilmington, Del., 1849-1896.

MISCELLANEOUS LETTERS to the Author.

NATIONAL ARCHIVES.—Early Records of the Bureau of Marine Inspection and Navigation.

POST OFFICE DEPARTMENT LIBRARY.—Memoranda covering records of postal contracts awarded to the B.S.P.Co.

* * *

Books, Pamphlets, and Special Articles Covering American
Steam Navigation.

ANON.—*Narrative of the loss of the Steam-Packet "Pulaski,"* Providence: H. H. Brown, 1839. (Pamphlet)

BALTIMORE STEAM PACKET COMPANY.—*An Act to Incorporate the Baltimore Steam Packet Company, passed 1839-40. Also acts of the General Assembly of Maryland supplementary thereto. Also the Act of 1922, By-Laws, April 4, 1930,* Baltimore: The Company, 1930. (Pamphlet)

BOWEN. See PARKER.

BRADLEE, FRANCIS G. B.—*Steam Navigation in New England,* Salem, Mass.: Essex Institute, 1920.

BROWN, ALEXANDER CROSBY.—*The Old Bay Line of the Chesapeake, A Sketch of a Hundred Years of Steamboat Operation,* in the *William and Mary Quarterly Magazine,* Williamsburg, Va., October, 1938. Reprinted as Publication No. 6 of The Mariners' Museum, Newport News, Va. (Pamphlet)

DAYTON, FRED ERVING.—*Steamboat Days,* New York: Stokes, 1925.

DUNBAR, SEYMOUR.—*A History of Travel in America,* 4 Vols., Indianapolis: Bobbs-Merrill, 1915.

GILFILLAN, S. COLOM.—*Early Steamboats of the Chesapeake,* in the Baltimore *Sun* Sunday Magazine, May 17, 1931, pp. 10-11.

HARDING, GARDNER.—*Save the Steamboat,* in the *Atlantic Monthly,* Boston, January, 1938.

HARDY, A. C.—*American Ship Types,* New York: Van Nostrand, 1927.

HARLAN AND HOLLINGSWORTH CORP.—*Semi-Centennial Memoire of the Harlan and Hollingsworth Company, 1836-1886,* Wilmington, Del., 1886.

ISHERWOOD, B. J.—*Experimental Researches in Steam Engineering,* 2 Vols., Philadelphia: Franklin Institute, 1863-5. (Vol. 2)

JENKINS, GEORGE (With A. E. WOODRUFF).—*The Fast Steamer "Florida,"* in the *International Marine Engineering,* New York, April, 1908, pp. 145-148.

LANTZ, EMILY EMERSON.—*History of the Steamboat on the Chesapeake,* in the Baltimore Sunday *Sun,* 1908. Particularly Article XII, *The Baltimore Steam Packet Company,* March 29, 1908, p. 15.

McADAM, ROGER WILLIAMS.—*The Old Fall River Line,* Brattleboro, Vermont: Stephen Daye, 1937.—*On the Old Fall River Line,* in *Travel,* New York, July, 1938, pp. 30-33, 47.—*Salts of the Sound,* Brattleboro, Vermont: Stephen Daye, 1939.

MACGREGOR, JOHN.—*Progress of America from the Discovery by Columbus to the Year 1846,* 2 Vols., London, 1847. (Vol. 2)

MARESTIER, J. B.—*Mémoire sur les Bateaux à Vapeur des États-Unis,* 2 parts, text and plates, Paris, 1824.

MEEKINS, LYNN R.—*Down the Bay to Norfolk,* in the Baltimore *American,* April 2, 1922, p. 4 D.

MERCHANTS AND MINERS TRANSPORTATION COMPANY.—*Tales of the Coast, a Brief History of the Company, 1852-1927,* Baltimore: Read-Taylor Press, 1927.

MORRISON, JOHN H.—*History of American Steam Navigation,* New York: W. F. Sametz, 1903.

PARKER, CAPT. HARRY. (With FRANK C. BOWEN).—*Mail and Passenger Steamships of the 19th Century,* Philadelphia: Lippincott, 1925.

RINGWALT, J. L.—*Transportation Systems in the United States,* Philadelphia, 1888.

ROSS, MAJOR OGDEN J.—*The Steamboats of Lake Champlain,* Champlain Transportation Co., 1930.—*The Steamboats of Lake George,* Lake George Steamboat Co., 1932.

SHANER, J. JEAN.—*Old Bay Line Gets Up Steam*, in the Baltimore Evening *Sun*, Feb. 19, 1940, p. 21.

SHANNAHAN, JOHN H. K.—*Steamboat'n' Days*, Baltimore: Norman Publishing Co., 1930.

STANTON, SAMUEL WARD.—*American Steam Vessels*, New York: Smith and Stanton, 1895.—*Baltimore and Norfolk Boats from the Early Days to the Present*, in the *Seaboard Magazine*, New York, June 16, 1892.

U. S. NAVY DEPARTMENT.—*Official Records of the Union and Confederate Navies in the War of the Rebellion*, Washington: Government Printer, 1894-1927. (Series I, Vols. 1-27; Series II, 1-3; Index.)

WALLACE, W. A.—*The "Great Eastern's" Log*, London: Bradbury and Evans, 1860.

WOODRUFF. See JENKINS.

* * *

Books, Pamphlets, and Special Articles Covering Local History of the Chesapeake Area.

ARTHUR, ROBERT.—*History of Fort Monroe*, Fort Monroe, Virginia: Coast Artillery School, 1930.

BALTIMORE AMERICAN.—*A History of the City of Baltimore, Its Men and Its Institutions*, Baltimore: The American, 1902.

BORUM, SAMUEL R.—*Norfolk Port and City*, Norfolk, 1893.

BURTON, HENRY W.—*The History of Norfolk, Virginia*, Norfolk, 1877.

ENOCH PRATT FREE LIBRARY.—*The Cator Collection of Baltimore Views, Catalogue of*, Baltimore: The Library, 1933. (Pamphlet)

FORREST, WILLIAM S.—*Historical and Descriptive Sketches of Norfolk and Vacinity*, Philadelphia: Lindsay & Blakiston, 1853.

GRIFFITH, T. W.—*The Annals of Baltimore*, Baltimore, 1833.

HOWARD, GEORGE W.—*The Monumental City*, Baltimore, 1873.

JONES, CARY W.—*Norfolk as a Business Centre*, Norfolk.

LAMB, ROBERT W.—*Our Twin Cities of the 19th Century, Norfolk and Portsmouth*, Norfolk: Barcroft, 1887-8.

LOSSING, BENSON J.—*The Pictorial Field Book of the Revolution*, New York: Harper & Bros., 1851-2.

MORDECAI, JOHN BROOKE.—*Travel and Communications*, Chapter XIV in *Richmond, Capital of Virginia, Approaches to Its History*, Richmond: Whittet & Shepperson, 1938.—*A brief history of the Richmond, Fredericksburg, and Potomac Railroad Company*, Richmond, 1940.

NORFOLK ADVERTISING BOARD.—*Through the Years in Norfolk*, Norfolk, 1936.

NOWITZKI, GEORGE I.—*Norfolk*, Norfolk, 1888.

POLLOCK, EDW.—*Sketch Book of Portsmouth, Va.,* Portsmouth, 1886.

PORTER, JOHN W. H.—*A Record of Events in Norfolk County, Va., from April 19, 1861, to May 10, 1862,* Portsmouth: W. A. Fiske, 1892.

SCHARF, COL. J. THOMAS.—*The Chronicles of Baltimore, being a complete history of Baltimore Town and Baltimore City,* Baltimore: Turnbull Bros., 1874.—*The History of Baltimore City and County,* Philadelphia, 1881.

STEINER, BERNARD C.—*Descriptions of Maryland,* Baltimore, The Johns Hopkins Press, 1904.—*Men of Mark in Maryland,* Washington, 1907. (Vol. 1, also Vol. 3 in same series by different author.)

STEWART, WILLIAM H.—*History of Norfolk County, Virginia,* Chicago, 1902.

WERTENBAKER, THOMAS JEFFERSON.—*Norfolk—Historic Southern Port,* Durham: Duke University Press, 1931.

Various City Directories of Baltimore and Norfolk. (W. S. FORREST, CHATAIGNE, WOODS, JOHN MURPHY, etc.)

* * *

Books, Pamphlets, and Special Articles Covering Travelers' Impressions, Guides, Etc., and Miscellaneous.

APPLETON'S *Illustrated Hand-Book of American Travel,* New York: Appleton, 1857.

COLCORD, JOANNA C.—*Songs of American Sailormen,* New York: W. W. Norton, 1939.

CRAM, MILDRED.—*Old Seaport Towns of the South,* New York: Dodd, Mead & Co., 1917. (pp. 43-51)

DEROOS, F. F.—*Personal Narrative of Travels in the United States in 1826,* London, 1827.

DICKENS, CHARLES.—*American Notes for General Circulation,* 2 Vols., London, 3rd Edition, 1842. (Vol. 2)

DUNLAP, WILLIAM, *Diary of, 1776-1839,* New York: New York Historical Society, 1931. (Vol. 2 of 3 Vols. and index)

HENGISTON, J. W.—*Something of Baltimore, Washington, the Chesapeake and Potomac,* in Colburn's *New Monthly Magazine,* London, 1853, Vol. 97, pp. 358-373.

JONES, CHARLES H. (Compiler).—*Appleton's Hand-Book of American Travel—Southern Tour,* New York: Appleton, 1874.

LLOYD, W. ALVIN.—*Steamboat and Railroad Guide,* New Orleans, 1857.

The Official Guide of the Railways and Steam Navigation Lines of the United States, Porto Rico, Canada, Mexico, and Cuba, New York: National Railway Publication Co., (Pub. Monthly), 72nd year, No. 10, Edition of March, 1940.

POWER, TYRONE.—*Impressions of America during the Years 1833, 1834, 1835,* 2 Vols., London, 1836. (Vol. 2)

ROBERTSON, WILLIAM (With W. F. ROBERTSON).—*Our American Tour: being a run of 10,000 miles from the Atlantic to the Golden Gate in the Autumn of 1869,* Edinburgh: Privately Printed, 1871.

WELD, CHARLES RICHARD.—*A Vacation Tour of the United States and Canada,* London, 1855.

WHALL, CAPT. W. B.—*Sea Songs and Shanties,* Glasgow: Brown, Son and Ferguson, 1910.

* * *

Advertising Material Published by the Baltimore Steam Packet Company.

ANON.—*The Marvelous Adventures of Captain John Smith—A Voyage to the Virginia Peninsulas,* Baltimore: Thomsen-Ellis Co., 1935.

The Bay Line News, A Weekly Newspaper published at Baltimore, May 15, 1926-May 21, 1927.

The Old Bay Line Magazine, edited by Alfred I. Hart. Baltimore, 1910-1918, monthly.

Via the Old Bay Line, Baltimore: King Printing Company, 1923. (Pamphlet)

Miscellaneous circulars, broadsides, leaflets, time-tables, menu cards, etc.

* * *

Ship Registers.

List of the Merchant Vessels of the United States, Washington, Government Printer, Annual Reports, 1868-1939.

Lloyd's Register of Shipping, London, Annual Reports.

Merchant Steam Vessels built in the United States, 1807-1856, Washington: U. S. Department of Commerce, Bureau of Navigation, 1931. (Mimeograph pamphlet)

New York Marine Register, a Standard Classification of American Vessels, New York: Root, Anthony & Co., 1857.

ROGERS AND BLACK.—*Marine Roll or List of Names Comprising the Mercantile Marine of the United States,* Baltimore: F. Lucas, Jr., 1847.

* * *

Periodicals.

Atlantic Monthly, Boston, January, 1938.

Colburn's *New Monthly Magazine,* London, 1853.

DeBow's *Commercial Review,* New Orleans.

Esquire, Chicago, March, 1940.

Federal Gazette and Baltimore Daily Advertiser, Baltimore.

Harper's Weekly, New York, 1857-.

Illustrated London News, London, 1845, 1875.

International Marine Engineering, New York, 1897-.

Manufacturers Record, August 21, 1896.

Municipal Journal, Baltimore,
"The Steamship Lines of Chesapeake Bay," Oct. 5, 1923.
"Activities of the Port of Baltimore," March 25, 1925.
"The *President Warfield,"* July 28, 1928.

Marine Review, Cleveland, Oct. 27, 1898, pp. 12-13. (S. S. *Tennessee*)

Marine Review, New York, April, 1935, p. 58. (*Seaboard,* freighter)

Nautical Gazette, New York. (Formerly *Seaboard Magazine*)

Niles' Weekly Register, Baltimore, 1811-.

Peoples Magazine, London, January 2, 1871.

Railway Age, New York, "S. Davies Warfield," Oct. 29, 1927, pp. 853-4. "L. R. Powell, Jr.", Nov. 26, 1927, pp. 1053-4.

Seaboard Magazine, New York. (Later *Nautical Gazette*)

U. S. Nautical Magazine, New York, 1854-.

William and Mary College Quarterly, Williamsburg.

* * *

Newspapers.

Baltimore *American and Commercial Daily Advertiser.*

Baltimore *News.*

Baltimore *News-Post.*

Baltimore *Sun.* (Morning, Evening and Sunday.)

New York *Dixon's Letter,* Supplement, 1842.

Norfolk *American Beacon,* 1815-.

Norfolk and Portsmouth *Herald.*

Norfolk *Argus.*

Norfolk *Virginian-Pilot.*

Petersburg *American Constellation.*

Portsmouth *Advertiser,* 1866-.

Portsmouth *Times and Commercial Advertiser.*

Richmond *Commercial Compiler.*

Richmond *Dispatch.*

Richmond *Enquirer.*

Richmond *Whig.*

Miscellaneous unidentified newspaper clippings owned by the Baltimore Steam Packet Company.

Various broadsides owned by the B.S.P.Co., the Pratt Library, The Mariners' Museum, etc.

Index